P9-ARY-105

New Directions for Teaching and Learning

Catherine M. Wehlburg
EDITOR-IN-CHIEF

Using the Decoding The Disciplines Framework for Learning Across the Disciplines

Janice Miller-Young
Jennifer Boman

EDITORS

Number 150 • Summer 2017
Jossey-Bass
San Francisco

Using the Decoding The Disciplines Framework for Learning Across the Disciplines
Janice Miller-Young, Jennifer Boman (eds.)
New Directions for Teaching and Learning, no. 150
Editor-in-Chief: *Catherine M. Wehlburg*

NEW DIRECTIONS FOR TEACHING AND LEARNING, (Print ISSN: 0271-0633; Online ISSN: 1536-0768), is published quarterly by Wiley Subscription Services, Inc., a Wiley Company, 111 River St., Hoboken, NJ 07030-5774 USA.
Postmaster: Send all address changes to *NEW DIRECTIONS FOR TEACHING AND LEARNING*, John Wiley & Sons Inc., C/O The Sheridan Press, PO Box 465, Hanover, PA 17331 USA.

Copyright and Copying (in any format)
Copyright © 2017 Wiley Periodicals, Inc., a Wiley Company. All rights reserved. No part of this publication may be reproduced, stored or transmitted in any form or by any means without the prior permission in writing from the copyright holder. Authorization to copy items for internal and personal use is granted by the copyright holder for libraries and other users registered with their local Reproduction Rights Organisation (RRO), e.g. Copyright Clearance Center (CCC), 222 Rosewood Drive, Danvers, MA 01923, USA (www.copyright.com), provided the appropriate fee is paid directly to the RRO. This consent does not extend to other kinds of copying such as copying for general distribution, for advertising or promotional purposes, for republication, for creating new collective works or for resale. Permissions for such reuse can be obtained using the RightsLink "Request Permissions" link on Wiley Online Library. Special requests should be addressed to: permissions@wiley.com

Information for subscribers
New Directions for Teaching and Learning is published in 4 issues per year. Institutional subscription prices for 2017 are:
Print & Online: US$454 (US), US$507 (Canada & Mexico), US$554 (Rest of World), €359 (Europe), £284 (UK). Prices are exclusive of tax. Asia-Pacific GST, Canadian GST/HST and European VAT will be applied at the appropriate rates. For more information on current tax rates, please go to www.wileyonlinelibrary.com/tax-vat. The price includes online access to the current and all online backfiles to January 1st 2013, where available. For other pricing options, including access information and terms and conditions, please visit www.wileyonlinelibrary.com/access.

Delivery Terms and Legal Title
Where the subscription price includes print issues and delivery is to the recipient's address, delivery terms are **Delivered at Place (DAP)**; the recipient is responsible for paying any import duty or taxes. Title to all issues transfers FOB our shipping point, freight prepaid. We will endeavour to fulfill claims for missing or damaged copies within six months of publication, within our reasonable discretion and subject to availability.

Back issues: Single issues from current and recent volumes are available at the current single issue price from cs-journals@wiley.com.

Disclaimer
The Publisher and Editors cannot be held responsible for errors or any consequences arising from the use of information contained in this journal; the views and opinions expressed do not necessarily reflect those of the Publisher and Editors, neither does the publication of advertisements constitute any endorsement by the Publisher and Editors of the products advertised.

Publisher: *NEW DIRECTIONS FOR TEACHING AND LEARNING* is published by Wiley Periodicals, Inc., 350 Main St., Malden, MA 02148-5020.

Journal Customer Services: For ordering information, claims and any enquiry concerning your journal subscription please go to www.wileycustomerhelp.com/ask or contact your nearest office.
Americas: Email: cs-journals@wiley.com; Tel: +1 781 388 8598 or +1 800 835 6770 (toll free in the USA & Canada).
Europe, Middle East and Africa: Email: cs-journals@wiley.com; Tel: +44 (0) 1865 778315.
Asia Pacific: Email: cs-journals@wiley.com; Tel: +65 6511 8000.
Japan: For Japanese speaking support, Email: cs-japan@wiley.com.
Visit our Online Customer Help available in 7 languages at www.wileycustomerhelp.com/ask

Production Editor: Poornita Jugran (email: pjugran@wiley.com).

Wiley's Corporate Citizenship initiative seeks to address the environmental, social, economic, and ethical challenges faced in our business and which are important to our diverse stakeholder groups. Since launching the initiative, we have focused on sharing our content with those in need, enhancing community philanthropy, reducing our carbon impact, creating global guidelines and best practices for paper use, establishing a vendor code of ethics, and engaging our colleagues and other stakeholders in our efforts. Follow our progress at www.wiley.com/go/citizenship

View this journal online at wileyonlinelibrary.com/journal/tl

Wiley is a founding member of the UN-backed HINARI, AGORA, and OARE initiatives. They are now collectively known as Research4Life, making online scientific content available free or at nominal cost to researchers in developing countries. Please visit Wiley's Content Access - Corporate Citizenship site: http://www.wiley.com/WileyCDA/Section/id-390082.html

Printed in the USA by The Sheridan Group.

Address for Editorial Correspondence: Editor-in-chief, Catherine M. Wehlburg, *NEW DIRECTIONS FOR TEACHING AND LEARNING*, Email: c.wehlburg@tcu.edu

Abstracting and Indexing Services
The Journal is indexed by Academic Search Alumni Edition (EBSCO Publishing); ERA: Educational Research Abstracts Online (T&F); ERIC: Educational Resources Information Center (CSC); Higher Education Abstracts (Claremont Graduate University); SCOPUS (Elsevier).

Cover design: Wiley
Cover Images: © Lava 4 images | Shutterstock

For submission instructions, subscription and all other information visit:
wileyonlinelibrary.com/journal/tl

FROM THE SERIES EDITOR

About This Publication

Since 1980, *New Directions for Teaching and Learning* (NDTL) has brought a unique blend of theory, research, and practice to leaders in postsecondary education. NDTL sourcebooks strive not only for solid substance but also for timeliness, compactness, and accessibility.

The series has four goals: to inform readers about current and future directions in teaching and learning in postsecondary education, to illuminate the context that shapes these new directions, to illustrate these new directions through examples from real settings, and to propose ways in which these new directions can be incorporated into still other settings.

This publication reflects the view that teaching deserves respect as a high form of scholarship. We believe that significant scholarship is conducted not only by researchers who report results of empirical investigations but also by practitioners who share disciplinary reflections about teaching. Contributors to NDTL approach questions of teaching and learning as seriously as they approach substantive questions in their own disciplines, and they deal not only with pedagogical issues but also with the intellectual and social context in which these issues arise. Authors deal on the one hand with theory and research and on the other with practice, and they translate from research and theory to practice and back again.

About This Volume

This volume provides examples and evidence of the various ways in which the Decoding the Disciplines framework has been applied across disciplines and used to inform teaching, curriculum, and pedagogical research initiatives at Mount Royal University. Chapters outline how various communities of practice got started, describe the analyses of three different collections of Decoding interviews, extend the Decoding framework using different theoretical lenses, and connect the learning to practical applications for teachers and teacher–scholars in higher education. The chapters provide detailed information so that readers from diverse backgrounds may develop effective models of practice for their own context and purposes.

Catherine Wehlburg
Editor-in-Chief

CATHERINE M. WEHLBURG *is the associate provost for institutional effectiveness at Texas Christian University.*

CONTENTS

EDITORS' NOTES

This special issue demonstrates how Decoding the Disciplines not only provides a framework for inquiry into teaching and learning disciplinary concepts but also holds much potential for bridging disciplinary thinking and teaching practice *across* disciplines and serving as a tool for both teaching and curriculum development. In Chapter 1, together with our Faculty Learning Community (FLC) coauthors, we describe the Decoding the Disciplines FLC at Mount Royal University, including how it started as a faculty development initiative and how it developed into various teaching, curriculum, and research projects that are presented in detail in subsequent chapters. We hope that others will use and extend this work to inform ways of thinking, practicing, and being for both teaching and learning in higher education.

Acknowledgment

The Academic Development Centre and the Institute for Scholarship of Teaching and Learning's TransCanada Collaborative Research Program, both at Mount Royal University, provided financial support for this work.

Janice Miller-Young
Jennifer Boman
Editors

JANICE MILLER-YOUNG was the director of the Institute for Scholarship of Teaching and Learning at Mount Royal University from 2013 to 2016. In this capacity, her work concentrated on developing and facilitating scholarship of teaching and learning initiatives across disciplines.

JENNIFER BOMAN is an associate professor and faculty development consultant in the Academic Development Centre at Mount Royal University. She has facilitated the Decoding the Disciplines Faculty Learning Community at Mount Royal. As a faculty development consultant, much of her work centers on supporting faculty in their teaching.

FOREWORD

You work on something for a long time and put it out for others to consider. You inevitably wonder: Will others grasp what you are trying to do? Will basic misunderstandings emerge that undermine the outcomes you are seeking, even when people believe that they are building on your work?

All of these concerns were on our minds when we began to publically present Decoding the Disciplines more than a decade ago. And that is why reading this volume has been such a joy. The truly impressive scholars of teaching and learning at Mount Royal University really got what we had been struggling to share. They got it and took this work in new directions that we had not explored.

Decoding the Disciplines emerged from the Indiana University Freshman Learning Project (FLP), a program designed to help instructors increase learning in their courses. Neither a method of instruction per se nor an abstract exploration of the nature of a discipline, Decoding provides a framework for identifying and remedying those elements of a course that are most problematic for students. From the FLP there emerged a seven-step process in which instructors identify a bottleneck to learning, make explicit the mental operations required to overcome the obstacle, model the required steps for students, give them practice at these skills, deal with any emotional bottlenecks that interfere with learning, assess the success of their efforts, and share the results. What began as a program focused on learning issues on a particular campus was transformed into a vehicle for the scholarship of teaching and learning with the publication of *Decoding the Disciplines* in an earlier issue of *New Directions for Teaching and Learning* and with the creation of the History Learning Project with Arlene Díaz and Leah Shopkow.

Decoding is now being explored by teams in at least ten countries, but none of these have done more to realize its potential than the instructors and educational developers who created this volume. In the early development of the Decoding paradigm we concentrated, of necessity, on relatively concrete and practical issues. Leah Shopkow added a greater theoretical

New Directions for Teaching and Learning, no. 150, Summer 2017 © 2017 Wiley Periodicals, Inc.
Published online in Wiley Online Library (wileyonlinelibrary.com) • DOI: 10.1002/tl.20243

dimension to this work with her explorations of the ways in which student misunderstandings of the epistemological orientations of particular disciplines could block learning. But we have not had the opportunity to fully explore the theoretical foundations of this work. Focusing on the second step in the process—making explicit the mental operations students must master—the group at Mount Royal has built on previous work and taken the model in entirely new directions. Their systematic, qualitative analysis of the Decoding interviews is a model for future work in this field, as is their application of phenomenology, hermeneutics, and identity theory to Decoding.

Second, they have made great contributions to our understanding of the mental operations that transcend disciplinary boundaries. In developing Decoding, we avoided too much discussion of shared patterns across fields, because of the danger that instructors would lose focus on the particular mental operations required in their courses in search for vague and generic patterns of critical thinking. But there are commonalities across disciplines that need to be explored systematically. This volume does just that, providing a model for the analysis of similar patterns of operating that must be mastered in multiple fields.

Next the Mount Royal group has focused on areas that had previously received less attention in Decoding—professional education and curriculum. They have realized that in these areas students need to master not only academic knowledge but also the patterns of actions and reactions that occur in a professional setting. They transformed their curriculum by using Decoding to unpack professional intuition and disrupt non-evidence-based practices. Their efforts open up valuable areas for future work.

Finally, the work of this team provides a marvelous example of the collaborative nature of Decoding. From its beginning the paradigm has built upon interaction of faculty across disciplines, because encountering the basic operations in other fields is a crucial element in recognizing those in one's own. Using Decoding the Disciplines as the guiding process in Faculty Learning Communities motivates instructors to dig deeply into the nature of their disciplines and to find creative ways to share it with their students. That power is visible in every page of this volume. Whether they are exploring the dimensions of professional education or considering how best to help students build a bridge in Honduras, the authors are using to great advantage the emotional energy and insights generated by being part of a team. Thus, although this volume concentrates on the second step of Decoding, it is also a marvelous example of the seventh step—sharing.

This book is a wonderful place to begin an exploration of the rapidly expanding Decoding paradigm. The reader can move from here to discussions of the other steps of the process and to alternatives to the interview process through the works mentioned in the notes or in our recent books (David Pace, *The Decoding the Disciplines Paradigm: Seven Steps to Increased Student Learning*, Indiana University Press, and Joan Middendorf and Leah

Shopkow, *Decoding the Disciplines: How to Help Students Learn Critical Thinking*). But the work of the team at Mount Royal University represents a major contribution to the development of Decoding the Disciplines, and instructors from all fields will find this work enlightening.

David Pace
Joan Middendorf

DAVID PACE is an emeritus professor of European History at Indiana University, a co-founder of the Freshman Learning Project, and the president of the International Society for the Scholarship of Teaching and Learning in History.

JOAN MIDDENDORF is Lead Instructional Consultant at the Center for Innovative Teaching and Learning and Adjunct Professor in Educational Leadership at Indiana University, where she developed the "Decoding the Disciplines" approach along with David Pace.

NEW DIRECTIONS FOR TEACHING AND LEARNING • DOI: 10.1002/tl

1

In this chapter we describe the Decoding the Disciplines Faculty Learning Community at Mount Royal University and how Decoding has been used in new and multidisciplinary ways in the various teaching, curriculum, and research projects that are presented in detail in subsequent chapters.

Overview of Decoding across the Disciplines

Jennifer Boman, Genevieve Currie, Ron MacDonald, Janice Miller-Young, Michelle Yeo, Stephanie Zettel

The Decoding the Disciplines Faculty Learning Community at Mount Royal University consists of a core group of six faculty members who came together to further understand and investigate how to make disciplinary ways of thinking and knowing more explicit to learners. The group's original goal was to interrogate the Decoding the Disciplines model (Pace and Middendorf 2004) and to consider how this framework might be used within our own contexts. The Decoding model suggests that teachers, operating as experts in their disciplines, hold tacit knowledge and implicit ways of thinking that are not accessible to novices in the discipline. Consequently, teachers and students may notice bottlenecks—areas in the discipline where students get stuck in their learning. A key step toward addressing the bottlenecks is a Decoding interview in which teachers uncover and unpack crucial mental operations. The interview can yield important insights for teachers who want to make their mental processes visible to students in order to help facilitate students' movement through the bottlenecks.

As a learning community, our group began conducting Decoding interviews with one another and analyzing the resulting dialogues. We went beyond cognitive bottlenecks, for which Decoding has typically been used, to include epistemological and ontological bottlenecks (Miller-Young and Boman, Chapter 2). In doing so, we explored new lines of questioning and found rich themes about expert disciplinary thinking. These themes illuminated the complexity of the expert teachers' thinking and helped us understand why the bottlenecks were so challenging for students. We wanted to share these insights with colleagues at our institution and, thus, our work expanded over time to include outreach to increase other faculty members'

NEW DIRECTIONS FOR TEACHING AND LEARNING, no. 150, Summer 2017 © 2017 Wiley Periodicals, Inc.
Published online in Wiley Online Library (wileyonlinelibrary.com) • DOI: 10.1002/tl.20234

awareness and use of the Decoding model. We have also provided support for those using the Decoding process for purposes such as curriculum revision and individual development of teaching. The following overview provides a summary of the group's work and sets the context for the articles to follow.

The Decoding the Disciplines Faculty Learning Community

How does a group of interested faculty members come together for the common purpose of increasing their understanding of how students learn disciplinary ways of thinking? In this case, the group emerged organically out of a related faculty development initiative. Each year the university's teaching support center offers a series of yearlong Faculty Learning Communities (FLCs) on a variety of topics. In 2011–2012, a group of eight faculty members and a facilitator (a faculty developer working in the center) came together to explore and study theories and practices related to assessment. Part of our conversation and reading included an in-depth exploration of outcomes-based assessment (Driscoll and Wood 2007). From these discussions, it became apparent to us that in order to make our assessments more transparent to students, we needed to have a clearer picture of the mental operations we expected students to learn. In other words, we needed to unpack the complex skills and outcomes that we were attempting to assess so that we could make them explicit and visible to students. We grappled with a key question: How could we uncover hidden assumptions and tacit thinking in our assessments?

At the conclusion of the yearlong FLC on assessment, a core group of four participants decided to continue the conversation about uncovering expert thinking in assessment and teaching using the Decoding the Disciplines model. We invited two additional, interested faculty members to join our group. We began our learning community by reading the Decoding literature as well as other related sources (for example, *Making Thinking Visible*, Ritchhart, Church, and Morrison 2011). Several members of our group also attended the International Society for the Scholarship of Teaching and Learning (ISSOTL) conference to participate in a Decoding workshop (Middendorf, Pace, Shopkow, and Díaz 2012). Throughout these experiences, we were struck by the power of the Decoding interview in revealing basic assumptions about disciplinary thinking.

After the instructor has identified a bottleneck where students get stuck in their learning, the next step in the Decoding process is an interview (Middendorf and Pace 2004). The primary task of the Decoding interview is to identify how the instructor approaches the bottleneck by making explicit what is intuitive, hidden, or automatic for her as an expert. This goal is typically accomplished using two interviewers who are not familiar with the subject matter and can act as novices in the discipline. The central question that they ask with respect to how the instructor addresses the bottleneck is, How do you do that? (Middendorf and Rehrey 2008). Middendorf and Pace (2004) describe this process for the interviewee as the "most intellectually demanding of all the steps in the Decoding the Disciplines approach" (5). The interviewee may experience discomfort as they realize that they cannot readily articulate their thinking and that perhaps they have not provided clear explanations to students. In fact, this "aha" moment or instance where the expert herself struggles to deconstruct her intellectual process is a signal that the interview is on the right track (Middendorf and Rehrey 2008).

Our faculty learning community was intrigued by the role of the Decoding interview in uncovering disciplinary mental operations that were hidden not only from students but also from the expert himself. Although there were general guidelines on the types of questions that help prompt the interviewee to reconstruct how he approaches the bottleneck (Middendorf and Rehrey 2008), the literature on the Decoding interviewing process was scarce. We wanted to better understand how the interviews unfolded to reveal expert disciplinary thinking. We decided that the best approach was to "learn by doing" and made a plan to conduct Decoding interviews with one another and to record and transcribe the interviews so that we could examine the resulting dialogues.

The Decoding Interviews

Our group conducted the first Decoding interview as a group; all members of the group interviewed one of our group members. As this interview progressed, we quickly realized the challenge of staying true to the purpose of the interview—that is, talking about how the expert accomplishes a particular bottleneck rather than talking about teaching. With practice, we were able to more successfully direct the expert to talk about his or her own thinking processes and leave the discussions about teaching and how to model these operations for students for follow-up conversations. A second challenge that we encountered as we moved further into our interviews with one another was that not that all interviewees presented cognitive or procedural bottlenecks. Some presented epistemological or ontological bottlenecks (Miller-Young and Boman, Chapter 2) that, for us, proved to be more difficult to deconstruct.

During the time that we were conducting interviews, we invited David Pace to speak at our campus. The purposes of the visit were twofold. First, we asked him to consult with us and give us feedback about our firsthand experiences conducting Decoding interviews. Second, we invited him to give a keynote presentation and workshops to introduce faculty members at our institution to the Decoding model. Following his visit, we invited any interested participants to engage in a Decoding interview with us as a faculty development initiative. We offered to conduct the interview with them and

NEW DIRECTIONS FOR TEACHING AND LEARNING • DOI: 10.1002/tl

to follow up with discussions about how to apply what they learned during the interview to their teaching.

Our Decoding learning community continued to meet to discuss what we had learned from engaging in the interviewing process. Despite interviewing participants from different disciplines and who had different kinds of bottlenecks, we began to notice similar themes appearing across several interviews. For example, one idea that we saw in multiple interviews was the idea of withholding or waiting. A characteristic of expert thinking that we observed was that experts held back and paused in their disciplinary thinking. In contrast, the experts described their students as rushing ahead to judgment. Although we had learned much about the interviewing process from conducting our interviews, we also realized we had rich dialogues that held a lot of learning about expert disciplinary thinking. We obtained ethical approval to use our data for research and contacted participants to seek permission to include their transcripts in the analysis.

We conducted an in-depth qualitative analysis of interviews with seven disciplinary experts from four diverse disciplines. Each instructor chose a unique bottleneck that represented a cognitive, epistemological, or ontological block that their students were encountering. The themes in expert disciplinary thinking arising from these interviews are described in Chapter 2 (Miller-Young and Boman). Three subsequent chapters also present further analyses of these interviews through three different lenses. In Chapter 3, Currie uses phenomenology to interrogate the concept of embodiment in the interviews. In Chapter 4, Yeo presents a hermeneutic analysis of the interviews to describe how some interviewees expressed an understanding of their discipline. Finally, in Chapter 5, MacDonald uses the lens of identity theory to discuss how the interviewees inserted professional identity elements into their narratives.

Decoding in Practice: Applications of the Decoding Model

Although the initial goal of our faculty learning community was to investigate how to make our own tacit disciplinary knowledge more explicit to our students, our process expanded over time to support others in the university community who were interested in using the Decoding model. One such example is a multidisciplinary group of faculty teaching with community service-learning pedagogy. The group was about to engage in a collaborative self-study of their experiences in teaching global service-learning courses and were particularly interested in how this experience shaped their understanding and learning about reciprocity. One of the members from our Decoding learning community presented the Decoding framework to them and they subsequently elected to use the Decoding interviews as one method of data collection in their self-study. The Decoding faculty learning community assisted in the interviewing process. Their analysis found that the Decoding interview played an important role in developing the

NEW DIRECTIONS FOR TEACHING AND LEARNING • DOI: 10.1002/tl

community and trust necessary for the study to generate new knowledge (Miller-Young et al. 2015); they further explore their multidisciplinary self-study process and its impact on their practice in Chapter 6.

The Decoding the Disciplines framework has also been used in several departments across campus for the purposes of curriculum redesign. Faculty in the journalism program used it to inform program redesign and the results from Decoding interviews also informed the redesign of a combined biology and nursing course. Most recently, the athletic therapy program has used Decoding interviews about multiple bottlenecks within a program to provide the athletic therapy instructors with information to inform their curriculum change toward a competency-based model. Yeo and colleagues describe their curriculum transformation process and the role of Decoding interviews in Chapter 7.

Looking Forward

McKinney (2013, 3) called for "more resources that offer examples, applications and discussions of critical issues of SoTL [scholarship of teaching and learning] in disciplines beyond our own and in interdisciplinary SoTL efforts. Such resources help broaden our horizons and encourage cross-disciplinary collaborations by sharing conceptual frameworks, methodologies, key results and practical applications that may be useful in our own classrooms and SoTL research." In the same collection, Poole (2013) argues that diverse methodologies and theoretical perspectives should be used to study teaching and learning. In this special issue of *New Directions for Teaching and Learning*, we answer these calls by demonstrating how the Decoding the Disciplines framework holds much potential for bridging disciplinary thinking and teaching practice across disciplines. The following chapters represent applications of the Decoding model in various scholarly and applied contexts. In addition, in Chapter 8, we synthesize these findings and provide recommendations for how the Decoding framework can be used in other contexts. We hope that these examples will help readers to consider ways in which they might identify and translate the crucial ways of thinking, practicing, and being in their own disciplines in order to improve student learning.

References

Driscoll, Amy, and Swarup Wood. 2007. *Developing Outcomes-Based Assessment for Learning-Centered Education: A Faculty Introduction*. Sterling, VA: Stylus.

McKinney, Kathleen. 2013. "Introduction to SoTL in and across the Disciplines." In *The Scholarship of Teaching and Learning in and across the Disciplines*, edited by Kathleen McKinney, 1–11. Bloomington: Indiana University Press.

Middendorf, Joan, and David Pace. 2004. "Decoding the Disciplines: A Model for Helping Students Learn Disciplinary Ways of Thinking." In *New Directions for Teaching and Learning: No. 98. Decoding the Disciplines: Helping Students Learn Disciplinary Ways of*

Thinking, edited by David Pace and Joan Middendorf, 1–12. San Francisco: Jossey-Bass.

Middendorf, Joan, David Pace, Leah Shopkow, and Arlene Díaz. *Decoding the Disciplines: Getting Through Bottlenecks and Thresholds*. Workshop presented at The International Society for the Scholarship of Teaching & Learning Conference, Hamilton, Ontario, Canada, October 2012.

Middendorf, Joan, and George Rehrey. *Developing an Evidence-Based Curriculum and Assessment: The History Learning Project*. Paper presented at the Professional and Organizational Development Network Conference, Reno, NV, October 2008.

Miller-Young, Janice, Yasmin Dean, Melanie Rathburn, Jennifer Pettit, Margot Underwood, Judy Gleeson, Roberta Lexier, Victoria Calvert, and Patti Clayton. 2015. "Decoding Ourselves: An Inquiry into Faculty Learning About Reciprocity in Service-Learning." *Michigan Journal of Community Service Learning* 22 (1): 32–47.

Pace, David, and Joan Middendorf, eds. 2004. *New Directions for Teaching and Learning: No. 98. Decoding the Disciplines: Helping Students Learn Disciplinary Ways of Thinking*. San Francisco: Jossey-Bass.

Poole, Gary. 2013. "Square One: What Is Research?" In *The Scholarship of Teaching and Learning in and across the Disciplines*, edited by K. McKinney, 135–151. Bloomington: Indiana University Press.

Ritchhart, Ron, Mark Church, and Karin Morrison. 2011. *Making Thinking Visible: How to Promote Engagement, Understanding, and Independence for All Learners*. New York: John Wiley & Sons.

JENNIFER BOMAN *has been a faculty developer and faculty member in Mount Royal University's Academic Development Centre since 2010.*

GENEVIEVE CURRIE *has been a faculty member at Mount Royal University since 2001 and teaches within the School of Nursing and Midwifery.*

RON MACDONALD, *now retired, was a college and university teacher of political science, political philosophy, and journalism for 35 years. He was a working journalist for 30 years.*

JANICE MILLER-YOUNG *was the director of the Institute for SoTL at Mount Royal University from 2013 to 2016 and is now a Professor and the Academic Chair of the Centre for Teaching and Learning at the University of Alberta.*

MICHELLE YEO *has been a faculty developer and faculty member in Mount Royal University's Academic Development Centre since 2007.*

STEPHANIE ZETTEL *has been a full-time faculty member in Mount Royal University's School of Nursing and Midwifery since 2009 and before that taught in the clinical environment as part-time faculty since 2002.*

2

This chapter presents the bottlenecks identified by seven faculty members from diverse disciplines and an inductive content analysis of their Decoding interviews. Representative quotations illustrate themes in the interviews and we consider the implications for both faculty development and pedagogical research.

Uncovering Ways of Thinking, Practicing, and Being through Decoding across Disciplines

Janice Miller-Young, Jennifer Boman

Decoding the Disciplines is a process designed to help instructors and educational consultants articulate expert approaches to difficult, or "bottleneck," concepts and to find new ways to help students learn these concepts (Pace and Middendorf 2004). After identifying a bottleneck, the process continues with an interview that helps the instructor better articulate his or her own thinking in order to model it for students. Most Decoding work has focused on procedural and cognitive bottlenecks in specific disciplines such as humanities, history, and geology (e.g., Ardizzone, Breithaupt, and Gutjahr 2004; Shopkow et al. 2013; Zhu et al. 2012). The related scholarship has typically described pedagogical changes and resulting learning outcomes for students, with less attention given to the commonalities in themes that emerge across groups of experts. In the following chapter we demonstrate how there is much to be learned by looking more closely at what Decoding interviews can uncover through applying the Decoding framework across disciplines.

Because the focus of most Decoding scholarship to date has been primarily on student outcomes, there is little written about the Decoding interview process itself. Pace and Middendorf (2004) describe the interview as intellectually demanding for the interviewee. They recommend that interviewers should keep the focus on the interviewee's thinking process, use questions such as "How do you do that?," probe at the place where the interviewee cannot explain, and summarize their thinking back to them at an abstract level (Shopkow, Diaz, and Pace 2013). In one example from the History Learning Project, Shopkow (2010) used interview excerpts to illustrate how the interview process can push faculty to recognize their own

New Directions for Teaching and Learning, no. 150, Summer 2017 © 2017 Wiley Periodicals, Inc.
Published online in Wiley Online Library (wileyonlinelibrary.com) • DOI: 10.1002/tl.20235

tacit knowledge and generate surprising realizations that what is simple and self-evident for them is likely not so for students. This dearth of literature about the Decoding interview itself was one reason we set about to practice and study the interview process and outcomes.

Decoding work has primarily focused on procedural and cognitive processes, and its utility in decoding other types of bottlenecks and in multidisciplinary contexts has only begun to be explored. Shopkow (2010) used Decoding interviews of cognitive and procedural bottlenecks in history to demonstrate that epistemological and emotional bottlenecks may also be unearthed and that the conceptual and ontological are inextricably linked. Similarly, Middendorf, Mickute, Saunders, Najar, Clark-Huckstep, and Pace (2015) write about revealing affective bottlenecks in history. In a multidisciplinary faculty self-study (Miller-Young et al. 2015) participants explored the utility of using the Decoding interview for studying faculty learning about reciprocity in service-learning. By analyzing each others' interviews within their community of practice, they found the Decoding interview to be useful not only in uncovering participants' thinking but also in generating new learning. Such work has demonstrated the value of more deeply analyzing the interviews in order to better describe the layers of complexity involved in the bottlenecks that teachers identify as well as the learning that is generated from the interviews. However, although there have been calls in the scholarship of teaching and learning (SoTL) literature for more interdisciplinary SoTL efforts (e.g., McKinney 2013), the Decoding the Disciplines framework has rarely been used for noncognitive bottlenecks or applied in an interdisciplinary way.

In separate but parallel work, the Thresholds Concepts movement also began with a disciplinary focus (Meyer 2008; Meyer and Land 2003, 2005). According to this framework, learning a threshold concept resembles passing through a portal, toward a transformed understanding. The original premise of their work was that threshold concepts are key concepts in a curriculum that students must master on their learning journey within a discipline. More recently, however, the threshold concepts framework has been applied to interdisciplinary concepts such as social justice (e.g., Kabo and Baillie 2010), environmental sustainability (e.g., Levintova and Mueller 2015), and becoming a researcher (e.g., Kiley and Wisker 2010). This work has generated rich, interdisciplinary conversations and debate as evidenced by the multiple conferences, articles, and edited volumes on the topic. One criticism, however, is that the movement invites instructors to examine their disciplines rather than their own teaching practice (Cousin 2007).

As with Threshold Concepts, the Decoding framework holds much potential for bridging disciplinary thinking and teaching practice across disciplines. In addition, the Decoding framework also engages teachers in critical reflection on their own thinking processes by beginning with the Decoding interview. The learning and insights that emerge during the interviewing process have obvious potential benefits for the individuals who participate in them but we suggest that sharing and integrating these insights can have benefits for others. In this chapter, we expand upon existing Decoding work in two ways: (1) interdisciplinary themes—we examine the common themes that emerge from Decoding interviews of faculty from four diverse disciplines; and (2) complexity of bottlenecks—we explore not only cognitive bottlenecks but also ones that we classify as epistemological and ontological, as described in the following section.

Background and Purpose of Study

As described in the previous chapter, Decoding interviews were conducted with faculty in the Decoding the Disciplines Faculty Learning Community as well as those who accepted our invitation to participate as part of a teaching development initiative. We conducted interviews with faculty from diverse disciplines and with teaching experience ranging from 10 to 30 years, about bottlenecks they identified. Interviews were transcribed and shared with the interviewees for further reflection. The interviews were often followed by discussions of possible teaching strategies to address the bottleneck. While conducting the interviews, our learning community began to notice common themes emerging across the interviews and decided to pursue a formal, in-depth analysis of the interview transcripts. We therefore asked permission from our interview participants to use their transcripts as data for this study. The research question explored in this chapter is What common themes emerge about expert disciplinary thinking in the Decoding interviews we have conducted?

Methods

Seven faculty members from four diverse disciplines and with different types of bottlenecks participated in the study. Their decoding interviews were qualitatively analyzed for common themes. This study was approved by the Mount Royal University Human Research Ethics Board.

Participants and Their Bottlenecks.   Four faculty members presented cognitive bottlenecks.

- *Louisa* identified that nursing students in her second-year pathophysiology class have a working knowledge of biological processes but have difficulty understanding how alterations in these processes manifest themselves as signs and symptoms in their patients.
- *Patricia*, an engineer teaching a first-/second-year dynamics class, noticed that students have trouble applying Newton's second law of motion ($F = ma$), especially in pulley problems where students tend to assume that the tension in a rope is equal to the weight of the object hanging from it (which is true only if the object is not accelerating).

New Directions for Teaching and Learning • DOI: 10.1002/tl

- **Bonnie**, a journalist, was concerned that senior journalism students continue to struggle with identifying and articulating good story ideas. In other words, her students not only struggle with identifying story ideas ("I just can't think of anything") but also with turning those ideas into journalism artefacts—stories—that an audience would benefit from in some way.
- **Colin**, a director and theatre instructor, wanted to help his acting students identify what he called the "super task," or as he explains, the "single thing that their character is trying to achieve as an overall, and overarching, purpose . . . The supertask is the linking glue that pulls all the pieces of the play together, and becomes an overall metaphor that the actor can hold inside of themselves."

One participant presented a bottleneck that was more epistemological, in other words, related to a misunderstanding of the nature of knowledge construction in the discipline.

- **Juan Carlos**, also a journalist, was concerned with his first-year students' beliefs in the necessity of objectivity in journalism. According to Juan Carlos, students will nod in agreement when presented with the objections to objectivity in class discussions and are shown examples of how the same set of facts differently arranged can lead to two different meanings, but in practice and in their own rhetoric later they revert to their own naive belief in objectivity.

Finally, two bottlenecks could be classified as ontological bottlenecks, as they were related to being and becoming a nurse. Ontology is one's view of reality and includes one's assumptions about the nature of reality and claims about what exists.

- **Monique** felt that her senior nursing students had difficulty understanding how to apply the nursing code of ethics in their practice. In particular, she noticed that although students may be able to "speak the language," they sometimes respond and react to things that shake them up (especially in their practicum experiences) in ways that indicate they haven't integrated the code of ethics into their practice.
- **Wendy** was concerned that her students "get stuck" with a mindset that nursing is about working in a hospital with people who are ill. In Wendy's community health/population course the bottleneck was the idea that the role of nursing is to keep people well so they never enter the hospital or so they are there for only a short time. Part of this role is understanding the determinants of health, which include income level and socioeconomic status, social supports, and educational level.

NEW DIRECTIONS FOR TEACHING AND LEARNING • DOI: 10.1002/tl

Interviews and Analysis.   At least two interviewers conducted each interview, which ranged in time from 54 to 102 minutes. The interviews were audio recorded and transcribed. The members of the faculty learning community then independently read the transcripts and met several times as a group to discuss their perceptions of the interviews and emerging themes. After these initial discussions, the authors of this chapter each independently and inductively coded for themes using the constant comparison method (Glaser 1965) and then discussed to reach consensus.

Findings: Common Themes

Common themes were collapsed into three main overarching categories: ways of thinking (i.e., deconstructing and reconstructing information and recognizing patterns), ways of practicing (i.e., valuing provisionality, expanding thinking, attending to the world, and taking agency), and ways of being (i.e., being ethical and authentic). Despite the variety of disciplines and types of bottlenecks presented, each of these themes was evident in over half of the interviews (Table 2.1).

The themes are described and illustrated with example quotes next.

Deconstructing/Reconstructing.   An initial theme that emerged from the participants' interviews was the idea that expert thinking involves both the deconstruction and reconstruction of knowledge. In other words, disciplinary thinking often involved both an analysis of individual parts and also a synthesis of the parts in order to examine the whole. Patricia spoke about this kind of thinking in engineering when she explained, "You have to break [the problem] down into the simple parts and look at each simple part by itself and then put it back together and solve the system of equations." Patricia went on to explain that an important component of her thinking in this regard is the judgment involved in knowing at which point to deconstruct the problem. Similarly, Louisa described that in her discipline of nursing, nurses must be prepared to think about and break problems down in different ways. She explained that nurses must think about their patients across many different levels, such as an organ level, a system level, a tissue level, and a cellular level. For Louisa, a key component of her expertise was her ability to move her thinking across these different levels of analysis in order to come to a clear picture of what was happening for a particular patient.

Like Louisa, Wendy, another nursing participant, also noticed that her disciplinary thinking involved a certain degree of analysis and deconstruction. She adopted the analogy of an onion and explained that she is able to peel back layers of a patient's immediate problem to reveal broader influences and determinants of health that may be influencing the situation. She suggested that although this kind of deconstruction of a problem is necessary to help identify possible routes to prevention, her students seemed unable to do that. In contrast, whereas Wendy's students struggled to

Table 2.1. Common Themes Identified in Six Decoding Interviews of Diverse Faculty Members and Diverse Bottlenecks

Themes		Cognitive				Epistemological	Ontological	
		Patricia	Bonnie	Louisa	Colin	Juan Carlos	Wendy	Monique
Ways of thinking	Deconstructing/reconsructing	✓		✓	✓	✓	✓	
	Recognizing patterns		✓	✓	✓	✓	✓	✓
Ways of practicing	Valuing provisionality	✓	✓		✓		✓	✓
	Expanding thinking		✓		✓	✓	✓	✓
	Attending to the world	✓	✓	✓	✓	✓	✓	✓
Ways of being	Taking agency		✓	✓	✓	✓	✓	✓
	Being ethical/ authentic		✓			✓	✓	✓

deconstruct a situation, Colin noted that in his discipline of theatre, students often struggled to reconstruct something to build new understandings. He reflected, "It is easy for me to actually show actors what the steps are, it is actually quite easy to show people how to take something apart; it is more difficult for them to understand, or then grasp after they have pulled something apart that it then all relates back together, because they become so interested in each piece individually." Indeed, Colin indicated that discovering the "linking force between all of the pieces" is a central component of actors' thinking.

Finally, although it might be expected that deconstructing and reconstructing information might be associated more with cognitive bottlenecks, we found evidence of this approach to knowing in Juan Carlos' interview as well. He explained:

> People are going out and gathering some facts and then are arranging them in a way that produces a meaning, but they could arrange them in a different way and produce a different meaning… We can have a bunch of true, verifiable facts; it is when we put them together in a meaningful arrangement that we depart from the one truth and we are actually imposing some sort of meaning. Any story is like that.

Juan Carlos emphasized the idea that meaning is subjective depending on how knowledge is arranged. Indeed, part of his bottleneck is coming to the realization that the meaning of a story may change as a result of reconstructing the elements in different ways.

Yeo further explores the dynamic to-and-fro between whole and part by analyzing Colin's, Louisa's, and Patricia's interviews using a hermeneutic lens (Chapter 4, this issue).

Recognition of Patterns.   The second way of thinking that participants spoke about was their ability to recognize patterns and to see connections and gaps among various pieces of information. Despite differences in their bottlenecks, two of the nursing participants both talked about relying on their knowledge of theory and research as well as their own experience in identifying patterns when diagnosing patients. Louisa explained:

> I would start first with looking at the signs and symptoms and see if there is a pattern with them… I can't put my finger on it, but I know [for the expert nurse] if there is something wrong and they know that the patient is going to go sour, and sure enough that patient goes sour even though they didn't have any clear indication, they can't back it up with any evidence, they just have a feeling because they have seen it with other patients, and that is when an expert is talking."

For Louisa, this form of pattern recognition was part of the expert's intuitive or implicit knowledge that she was trying to make more visible to her students, a difficulty in common with athletic therapy (Chapter 7, this issue).

Finally, both journalists also talked about recognizing patterns but for different reasons. Bonnie spoke about recognizing what makes a good story idea. She explained, "I get excited when the story doesn't fit what we consider to be a pattern of a predictable story ... it is like I am always classifying things and if it falls outside that kind of regular pattern, for whatever reason, to me it would seem worth exploring." Meanwhile, Juan Carlos offered a critical perspective on patterns in the broader discipline. He said,

> A lot of journalism is done on the spur of the moment and people tend to fall into interpretations that are already given ... no one is thinking very critically ... It is partly that we are all driven by ideology and we all have a perspective on the world that comes from our history, our class, location, our gender, our sexuality, all of these things make us situated in a particular way, and so we see things in a particular way.

For both Bonnie and Juan Carlos, it was important to recognize patterns so that they could also recognize and pursue more unique interpretations or angles.

For the participants who mentioned pattern recognition as an important way of knowing, a prerequisite seemed to be having adequate background knowledge in order to recognize what is new and what is old or to notice what is different. Being attentive to the world, one of the themes discussed later, outlines some of the ways in which the disciplinary experts seemed to acquire the necessary information and frameworks to be able to make these kinds of connections.

Valuing Provisionality.   In addition to speaking about ways of thinking in their disciplines, the participants also discussed ways of practicing in their disciplines. A key theme that emerged early in the analyses was the idea that the participants valued the importance of taking time when engaging in disciplinary thinking, a process that often involves waiting and withholding judgment before coming to a conclusion.

For example, Colin spoke of the provisional nature of the task of understanding the role of a character in a play. He described a process of continually rereading a play while remaining open and waiting for new insights about the characters to emerge. He suggested that "one of the hardest things I have to get young actors to do ... is not to make conclusions, to just keep on waiting for more information." In Colin's discipline, there is value in understanding the provisional nature of the task and trusting that one's understanding will deepen and broaden over time.

Similarly, in her discipline of engineering, Patricia spoke of the importance of not making assumptions and trusting the process when solving problems:

New Directions for Teaching and Learning • DOI: 10.1002/tl

Remember to draw the free body diagram and not just make that initial as-
sumption... the more and more complex these systems get, the more valuable drawing this out becomes... maybe that is [the source of the bottleneck],
that I recognize the fact that this is going to be valuable as the questions become more and more complicated and [the students] just haven't realized
that yet... I don't assume. If you are not told something, or something isn't
given in the question, don't assume. Don't assume the tension is equal to the
weight. Don't assume anything!

Wendy also spoke of the importance of not jumping to conclusions or
judgment in her discipline, nursing. She stated, "I try not to make assumptions and I try not to have already decided what is wrong with the person
before I have talked to them... You start and say 'How can I help you today? What would you like? What is the most important thing you want
me to focus on today?'" Wendy indicated that she had learned this process
of slowing down from observing her mentors. She noted, "They weren't
rushing—even though it was really busy."

This idea of being nonjudgmental and not rushing also emerged in
one of the journalism interviews. Bonnie spoke about the idea of allowing
time and space to fully consider her story ideas rather than making quick
judgments. What was common across the theme of valuing provisionality was participants' shared sense of the importance of waiting and being
open to possibilities rather than jumping to a foregone conclusion. As Yeo
(Chapter 4) describes, they exhibited an "openness to questions." The disciplinary experts clearly trusted the process of taking the time to think and
had the self-discipline to hold back from rushing in or making assumptions.

Expanding Thinking.   A second way of practicing, expanding thinking, refers to the idea of examining a problem or scenario from different points of view. This theme clearly related to the theme of valuing
provisionality because expanding thinking often requires pausing in order to more fully consider different perspectives. Similar to the sense of
being open and nonjudgmental in the previous theme, the purpose of
expanding thinking is not to reduce a situation to a binary or single answer but to be able to think about an issue in terms of the broader influences. When thinking is expanded, individuals are able to come to new
insights or perspectives and make sense of something through their own
experiences.

All three nursing participants spoke about the importance of expanding their thinking. Monique described her desire for students to learn to
examine situations from different angles. She stated that she wanted to see
her students "actually looking at the dilemma they are faced with and actually looking at different sides of it... there are multiple ways of looking at a
scenario... [I want them to have] a capacity to think critically with respect
and with a broader view." Wendy also spoke of the importance of encouraging thinking in terms of the big picture or broader view. She suggested

that in her own practice, "I continue to develop it...the art of asking those bigger questions, and the art of seeing that as the role of the nurse...to go bigger and broader. So not just conceptually we talk about it, but also how are you going to do this with your patients or the family so they get more comfortable with that?...it is to also consider the broader influences that have brought them to this place." Louisa, too, mentioned the importance expanding thinking and gathering a range of information so that you are then able to prioritize and "know what is foreground, know what is background." For the nursing participants, the ability to consider multiple perspectives and a broader view was an important component of disciplinary thinking.

Both journalism participants spoke to the possibilities that come from expanding thinking. When looking for story ideas, Bonnie indicated that she shifts into and out of different points of view and looks for missing perspectives such as "Who did [the reporter] not talk to?" She remarked, "Often what they miss is the face of the story." For Bonnie, examining multiple perspectives allowed her to identify gaps and potential opportunities. Juan Carlos mentioned the freedom that comes from moving beyond a particular way of thinking about or doing something. He mentioned that subjectivity in journalism is actually a "liberating idea because if you actually buy into this notion that there is no such thing as objectivity in this particular sense, then you are freed to make some conscious decisions about what kind of milieu you will develop in your reporting...you will be liberated from a lot of rules that constrict and confine you." Like the nursing participants, expanding thinking is an important way of practicing in the discipline.

Attentiveness to the World. Another theme that spoke to participants' ways of practicing was that they embodied a natural sense of curiosity and attentiveness to their environments. They did not just exist in their worlds—they were consciously aware of and engaged with their surroundings. For Louisa, attentiveness to the world included the sense of being "observant." She explained, "One of the questions I ask myself all the time is, 'What else do I want to know about this patient? What else will help me take care of him?'...a lot of it is being observant...I think that has really helped me in terms of understanding and gathering all the information that I need." For Louisa, being observant involved not only an attitude of inquisitiveness but also the practice of asking questions. Wendy agreed that observation and questioning were qualities she would like students to cultivate in their nursing practice.

In addition to questioning, participants described reading as a key practice in being attentive. For example, Wendy suggested, "one of our standards of practice is that we base care on evidence and so I know I need to do my research, I need to read and I need to be aware of what is out there and what the evidence is." Bonnie also spoke of the importance of reading. She mentioned,

[Students] don't seem to hear and see the things that I think as a journalist I hear and see . . . I am an avid consumer of news and so I stay abreast of what other people are doing in terms of news content, and in the way that I engage with that content in terms of story ideas is that I am constantly looking for— What do they cover? What are the gaps? What is it that follows? . . . I scan the newspaper every morning, my homepage is CBC and I am checking that site at least a couple of times in the day . . . and I will check what is going on in the Globe and Mail, Washington Post, New York Times through the week.

Juan Carlos agreed with Bonnie's need to be aware of the world and indicated, "I think I am pretty conscious of the general coverage around any given thing."

Finally, Patricia did not speak as explicitly about her attentiveness to the world but seemed to take it for granted. After describing the forces you feel when an elevator accelerates and decelerates, she was asked whether it was a natural process for her to analyze the mechanical things going on around her. She said "I don't know, not that I am really aware of, but if I felt something or saw something that seemed unusual I would notice that." She also talked about how, when calculating a quantity in an engineering problem "you get to your final answer—whatever it is that you are trying to figure out—and you go back to the question and look at it, 'Does that actually make sense?" It seemed that Patricia, like the other participants, had used her sense of curiosity and attentiveness to develop a framework of how the world works.

Taking Agency.   In addition to being attentive to the world, participants spoke of taking agency or moving forward in the world. Participants noted that the act of observing or noticing things often moved them toward action. For example, Monique explained, "When you noticed something was not quite right, and maybe that is a theory/practice sort of gap that you are living, when you kind of think, 'Yeah, this is not quite what we are talking about here. This was not what it was supposed to be' but then the question is how do you take the next step and what do you do? But I think for me it is just, 'Okay, this is not right and I need to do something.'" Wendy also spoke of the need to translate observations into actions. She commented, "When seeing the same person or the same issues again . . . try and think 'How can we prevent that? How can I set these people up so they are more prepared when they are discharged so they don't keep coming back again?"

This sense of agency was often coupled with the realization that taking action may include finding ways to move forward. For Louisa, sometimes moving forward meant relying on others' expertise. She explained, "In my practice when I was teaching on the unit, what I would do is take my case if it was something troubling and I didn't know, I would just look up the signs and symptoms and ask the experts that I was working with—because there is always somebody who knows more than you do, who can lend

you some expertise from their experience because they have seen more."
In journalism, Bonnie also talked about taking action by using her contacts
in order to move forward with a story idea. She indicated that she moved
forward with stories by asking a series of questions like "Who knows about
this? Who would know about this? How would I find out who knows about
this?"

Taking agency and moving forward may also involve a certain amount
of persistence and the courage and confidence to take risks. Bonnie identified that one difference between herself and her students was her willingness to connect with possible sources. She explained, "It is about having the
courage to just pick up the phone. It is like a cold call, right? ... I actually
pick up the phone a lot." She also noted the importance of having confidence in herself when pitching story ideas. She reflected, "Looking back to
my own practice ... it was confidence; I had the confidence to bring voice
to observations [that] I think had I lacked confidence I would have thought
sounded stupid."

Colin also noted that in theatre the idea of agency and moving forward
involves persistence and the willingness to try new approaches. He stated,

> There is a central idea within theatre and that I teach my students ... which
> is the idea of offer, so whenever you are at work in a scene you offer, and an
> offer can be ... it doesn't matter if an offer is turned down or accepted, because
> like you just offer something else, and you offer something else and you get
> very disconnected to ownership or self-worth in your offers, it is just about
> trying stuff—anything—because they know that is what is going to spur on
> the process.

For many of our experts, an important component of practicing in the
discipline is knowing how to move forward.

In Chapter 3, Currie further explores, through a phenomenological
lens, how these ways of practicing had been learned through lived experience, had become unconscious for faculty members, and how the Decoding
interview helped to increase their own awareness of their tacit expertise.

Ethics and Authenticity.   A final theme that emerged across the interviews was that of the expert being ethical and genuine in their practice.
Participants spoke about the need to be authentic and to have a critical
awareness of the impact of their actions on others.

Monique described her sense of ethics in nursing in this way:

> Well and this is why I think nursing is different from other disciplines be-
> cause it is not the safety, and I used to say it was the safety that makes this
> different ... it is actually the ethic, I think, that is different ... it goes back to
> would you want someone like this taking care of your family? ... I think it
> has something to do with a more fulsome view of ethics that is saying, "I want
> to know more."

NEW DIRECTIONS FOR TEACHING AND LEARNING • DOI: 10.1002/tl

Wendy also spoke about the importance of ethics in nursing. Like Monique, she felt that ethical practice included but went beyond immediate safety or competency concerns and involved figuring out how to work with others in an ethical, genuine, and respectful way.

Juan Carlos also identified a broader sense of ethical practice in his discipline of journalism. He spoke about the tension between the pressures of acquiring an audience but also needing to move forward with a particular perspective knowing that it may not be popular. He explained:

> Journalists want eyes on what they have done, and if they don't get eyes—or ears—on what they have done they have actually failed. Some of the things they might write at certain times just turned people off and they know it, and so do their editors. So there is nothing pure about that sort of thing and it is always infected by the commodification of journalism which I think now has reached a point where it is extreme, and it takes some considerable effort and courage to write and report against the grain.

Finally, the participants acknowledged that, although being ethical and genuine in their practice was something they strove for, it was not always an easy process and took time to develop. Bonnie reflected that how she practiced the ethics surrounding the search for story ideas was something that changed over time.

> It is a real negotiation if you are going to use first person sights and sounds as story observations, it is very challenging if you want to maintain trust in all those relationships ... I am not actively pumping my circle of friends for story ideas, although I think I did when I was younger ... which is plagued with problems. There were some personal costs there that I wish I had handled better.

Monique also spoke about the challenge involved in being ethical and genuine, from the perspectives of both the expert and the student. She noted, "Going back to the code of ethics, like it is sort of an authenticity that I think a lot of people aren't prepared to go to. We have to be vulnerable in order to understand vulnerability, that is what it comes down to."

For this group of disciplinary experts, being authentic and practicing in a manner that was principled and fair was not easy but seemed to be an important hallmark of being an expert in their chosen field and one that they wished to pass on to their students.

Discussion and Implications

The literature on expertise and teaching suggests that "expertise can sometimes hurt teaching because many experts forget what is easy and what is difficult for students" (Bransford, Brown, and Cocking 2000, 44).

Psychologists call this the curse of knowledge (Brown, Roediger, and McDaniel 2014). In this analysis, we can see how the bottlenecks identified by faculty members as being difficult for students are not necessarily simple concepts but actually require many different types of expert thinking that go beyond ways of thinking and practicing (Entwistle 2005) to include ways of being. Indeed, our interviews uncovered layers of complexity associated with each bottleneck, which our participants indicated, when pressed, that they had not truly understood until they either had years of professional experience or until they started teaching or both. Participants often left the interviews with a greater appreciation for the amount of time and experience required to become truly expert at addressing their bottlenecks. One participant, in her own article reflecting on the decoding process, said the process was a "game changer" (Haney 2015).

Although this study involved only a small group of faculty from four diverse disciplines, the findings support similar findings of expert–novice differences more broadly. For example, Shopkow (2010) showed that bottlenecks in learning history can be grouped into three categories related to the nature of the discipline and its practices, evidentiary practices and primary sources, and affective understandings and abilities (i.e., maintaining emotional distance, overcoming affective roadblocks, being willing to wait for an answer, and dealing with ambiguity). Wismath, Orr, and MacKay (2015) demonstrated that problem-solving skills in a liberal education science course require mental habits of patience and persistence, a valuing of understanding over determining the correct answer, and a realization of the importance of careful and complete modeling before "plunging in." Similarly, in design fields such as engineering, provisionality is part of practice; expert designers take an iterative and exploratory approach and consider many alternative approaches and solutions to a problem (Cross 2004). Indeed, research shows that, in general, experts have acquired "extensive knowledge that affects what they notice and how they organize, represent, and interpret information in their environment," which in turn improves their practice (Bransford, Brown, and Cocking 2000, 31).

It is useful to consider how the shared themes about expert disciplinary thinking apply to our own disciplines and how we can use these ideas to help inform how we approach bottlenecks to learning in our own teaching. In particular, our findings show how acquisition of knowledge and skills (ways of thinking) may be insufficient for mastering even the cognitive bottlenecks, let alone epistemological or ontological. Rather, as Dall'Alba (2009) argues, learning to be an expert occurs through integration of knowing, practicing, and being. If we conceptualize learning this way, we might consider whether our teaching decontextualizes knowledge from the practices to which it relates, whether we prioritize content and "efficiency of transmission" over deep understanding, and whether we focus on epistemology and narrow conceptions of knowledge at the expense of ontology. Similarly, these themes could inform curriculum planning and related teaching and learning research in one's course, program, or discipline. Finally, as Yeo, Currie, and MacDonald suggest in the following chapters, we might consider different lines of questions in the Decoding interview, particularly when interviewees get stuck and the interviewers might need to find another way to open the door into the expert's thinking process.

The advantage of the Decoding the Disciplines model is its engagement of the practitioner. We know that traditional research on pedagogy and novice–expert differences will not necessarily convince faculty members to change their teaching practice (e.g., Burn 2007; Singer, Nielsen, and Schweingruber 2012). In our study most participants, at some point in their interview, articulated a sudden and unprompted realization that describing their own thinking process or describing a personal experience that was influential to their own learning might be helpful for their students. In the words of Bonnie, "I have always really shied away from talking with students about my own practice. .... And yet as I talk to you [I realized] if done the right way maybe my students could benefit from my making those steps, if you will, a little clearer.... ... with these stories a little can go a long way." Although chapters 6 and 7 in this issue describe how the Decoding method has been used effectively in faculty-driven curriculum and research projects, our observations described here suggest that using the Decoding model has a potentially transformative effect on faculty teaching practice even if they are not actively involved in such a project as research or within a community of practice. For these reasons we suggest that the Decoding model holds much promise for a variety of faculty development initiatives as well as a method for pedagogical research.

References

Ardizzone, Tony, Fritz Breithaupt, and Paul C. Gutjahr. 2004. "Decoding the Humanities." In *New Directions for Teaching and Learning: No. 98. Decoding the Disciplines: Helping Students Learn Disciplinary Ways of Thinking*, edited by David Pace and Joan Middendorf, 45–56. San Francisco: Jossey-Bass.

Bransford, John D., Ann L. Brown, and Rodney R. Cocking. 2000. "How Experts Differ from Novices." In *How People Learn: Brain, Mind, Experience and School*, 31–35. Washington, DC: National Academies Press.

Brown, Peter C., Henry L. Roediger III, and Mark A. McDaniel. 2014. *Make It Stick: The Science of Successful Learning*. Cambridge, MA: Harvard University Press.

Burn, Katharine. 2007. "Professional Knowledge and Identity in a Contested Discipline: Challenges for Student Teachers and Teacher-Educators." *Oxford Review of Education* 33 (4): 445–467.

Cousin, Glynis. 2007. Exploring Threshold Concepts for Linking Teaching and Research. Paper presented at the International Colloquium: International Policies and Practices for Academic Enquiry, Winchester, United Kingdom.

Cross, Nigel. 2004. "Expertise in Design: An Overview." *Design Studies* 25 (5): 427–441.

Dall'Alba, Gloria. 2009. "Learning Professional Ways of Being: Ambiguities of Becoming." *Educational Philosophy and Theory* 41 (1): 34–45.

Entwistle, Noel. 2005. "Learning Outcomes and Ways of Thinking across Contrasting Disciplines and Settings in Higher Education." *Curriculum Journal* 16 (1): 67–82.

Glaser, Barney G. 1965. "The Constant Comparative Method of Qualitative Analysis." *Social Problems* 12 (4): 436–445.

Haney, Sally. 2015. "Interrogating Our Past Practice as We Scale the Walls of the Box We Call Journalism Education." In *Toward 2020: New Directions in Journalism Education*, edited by Gene Allen, Stephanie Craft, Christopher Waddell, and Mary Lynn Young, 64–81. Toronto: Ryerson Journalism Research Centre.

Kabo, Jens, and Caroline Baillie. 2010. "Engineering and Social Justice." In *Threshold Concepts and Transformational Learning*, edited by Jan H. F. Meyer, Ray Land, and Caroline Baillie, 303–315. Rotterdam, The Netherlands: Sense Publishers.

Kiley, Margaret, and Gina Wisker. "Learning to be a Researcher: The Concepts and Crossings." In *Threshold Concepts and Transformational Learning*, edited by Jan H. F. Meyer, Ray Land, and Caroline Baillie, 399–414. Rotterdam, The Netherlands: Sense Publishers.

Levintova, Ekaterina M., and Daniel Mueller. 2015. "Sustainability: Teaching an Interdisciplinary Threshold Concept through Traditional Lecture and Active Learning." *Canadian Journal for the Scholarship of Teaching and Learning* 6 (1).

Meyer, Jan H. F. 2008. *Threshold Concepts Within the Disciplines*. Rotterdam, The Netherlands: Sense Publishers.

Meyer, Jan H. F., and Ray Land. 2003. "Threshold Concepts and Troublesome Knowledge: Linkages to Ways of Thinking and Practicing Within the Disciplines." In *Improving Student Learning. Improving Student Learning Theory and Practice–10 years on*, edited by C. Rust, 412–424. Oxford: OCSLD.

Meyer, Jan H. F., and Ray Land. 2005. "Threshold Concepts and Troublesome Knowledge (2): Epistemological Considerations and a Conceptual Framework for Teaching and Learning." *Higher Education* 49 (3): 373–388.

Middendorf, Joan, Jolanta Mickute, Tara Saunders, José Najar, Andrew E. Clark-Huckstep, David Pace, with Keith Eberly and Nicole McGrath. 2015. "What's Feeling Got to Do with It? Decoding Emotional Bottlenecks in the History Classroom." *Arts and Humanities in Higher Education* 14 (2): 166–180.

Miller-Young, Janice, Yasmin Dean, Melanie Rathburn, Jennifer Pettit, Margot Underwood, Judy Gleeson, Roberta Lexier, Victoria Calvert, and Patti Clayton. 2015. "Decoding Ourselves: An Inquiry into Faculty Learning About Reciprocity in Service-Learning." *Michigan Journal of Community Service Learning* 22 (1): 32–47.

McKinney, Kathleen, ed. 2013. *The Scholarship of Teaching and Learning in and across the Disciplines*. Bloomington, IN: Indiana University Press.

Pace, David, and Joan Middendorf, eds. 2004. *New Directions in Teaching and Learning: No. 98. Decoding the Disciplines: Helping Students Learn Disciplinary Ways of Thinking*. San Francisco: Jossey-Bass.

Shopkow, Leah. 2010. "What Decoding the Disciplines Can Offer Threshold Concepts." In *Threshold Concepts and Transformational Learning*, edited by Jan H. F. Meyer, Ray Land, and Caroline Baillie, 317–331. Rotterdam, The Netherlands: Sense Publishers.

Shopkow, Leah, Arlene Diaz, Joan Middendorf, and David Pace. 2013. "The History Learning Project 'Decodes' a Discipline: The Union of Research and Teaching." In *Scholarship of Teaching and Learning in and across the Disciplines*, edited by Kathleen McKinney, 93–113. Bloomington, IN: Indiana University Press.

Shopkow, Leah, Arlene Diaz, and David Pace. 2013. Decoding the Disciplines: Student Difficulties and Disciplinary Ways of Knowing. Paper presented at the Teaching Professor Conference, New Orleans, LA.

Singer, Susan R., Natalie R. Nielsen, and Heidi A. Schweingruber, eds. 2012. *Discipline-Based Education Research: Understanding and Improving Learning in Undergraduate Science and Engineering*. Washington, DC: National Academies Press.

Wismath, S., Doug Orr, and Bruce MacKay. 2015. "Threshold Concepts in the Development of Problem-Solving Skills." *Teaching and Learning Inquiry* 3 (1): 63–73.

Zhu, Chen, George Rehrey, Brooke Treadwell, and Claudia C. Johnson. 2012. "Looking Back to Move Ahead: How Students Learn Geologic Time by Predicting Future Environmental Impacts." *Journal of College Science Teaching* 41(3): 60–66.

JANICE MILLER-YOUNG *is a professor and the academic chair of the Centre for Teaching and Learning at the University of Alberta.*

JENNIFER BOMAN *has been a faculty developer and faculty member in Mount Royal University's Academic Development Centre since 2010.*

3

This chapter describes how seven disciplinary bottlenecks from four diverse disciplines were analyzed using a phenomenological perspective and includes a discussion of embodied knowing and implications for educators.

Conscious Connections: Phenomenology and Decoding the Disciplines

Genevieve Currie

If I were to tell you where my greatest feeling . . . of my earthly existence has been, I would have to confess: It has always, here and there, been in this kind of in-seeing, in the indescribably swift, deep, timeless moments of . . . seeing into the heart of things.

Rilke (1987)

Introduction

Decoding the Disciplines is a process to increase student learning by helping educators to unpack complex disciplinary knowledge (Pace and Middendorf 2004). As described by Boman, Currie, MacDonald, Miller-Young, Yeo, and Zettel (Chapter 1), a team of researchers began as a Faculty Learning Community (FLC) and studied the Decoding process over 2 years. The FLC interviewed each other in a series of Decoding the Disciplines interviews and eventually opened up this opportunity for other faculty at our university. Participants were invited to identify a bottleneck, which Pace and Middendorf (2004) describe as a phenomenon or concept that students struggle with and are unable to successfully understand to move forward in thinking and discovery. The interviewees and their bottlenecks are described in detail in Chapter 2, where an inductive analysis of the interviews elicited many common themes, which were classified into ways of thinking, ways of practicing, and ways of being. Chapters 4 and 5 in this issue explore the interviews from hermeneutic and identity theory perspectives. After reading and reviewing the interviews I chose the method of phenomenology as a "meaning-giving method of inquiry" (Van Manen 2014, 16) to

New Directions for Teaching and Learning, no. 150, Summer 2017 © 2017 Wiley Periodicals, Inc.
Published online in Wiley Online Library (wileyonlinelibrary.com) • DOI: 10.1002/tl.20236

understand the interviewees' texts on disciplinary knowledge surrounding ways of practicing.

Phenomenology influences a thoughtful attentive practice by revealing the meanings of human experience and is concerned with the study of life as we experience it (Van der Zalm and Bergum 2000). This type of inquiry makes life experience more conscious (Polkinghorne 1983). Through reflection on the transcribed interviews, I became aware that the elements of a phenomenological perspective shed light on ways of practicing, particularly in terms of the lived experience of acquiring disciplinary knowledge, embodied knowing, and prereflective practice. The Decoding interviews helped participants to reveal the lived experience of acquiring disciplinary knowledge. The method of phenomenology as a system of inquiry (Van Manen 2014) is explored in terms of how it can be applied to the Decoding process. I then use this perspective to consider lived experience, prereflective practice, and embodiment that were uncovered during the Decoding interviews and conclude with implications for educators.

Phenomenology as a Method of Inquiry

Phenomenology is a philosophical method of inquiry that studies the structure of experience and consciousness experienced by individuals in everyday life (Smith 2013). Phenomenology can reveal practical forms of behavior and actions as they appear through consciousness and describes and interprets these experiences to "unfold meanings" as they are lived in everyday existence (Laverty 2003, 4). Phenomenologists believe that to be human is to be embedded and immersed in the world, and an understanding of life experience is based on a process that is contextual, subjective, intersubjective, and evolving (Merleau-Ponty 1945). Phenomenology is interested in getting to the descriptive heart of a particular experience, to its essence. In Van Manen's (1990) terms, "a good phenomenological description that constitutes the essence of something is construed so that the structure of a lived experience is revealed to us in such a fashion that we are now able to grasp the nature and significance of this experience in a hitherto unseen way" (39).

The phenomenological lenses of the philosophers Merleau-Ponty and Van Manen are used in this chapter to describe and interpret the conscious and unconscious experience within ways of practicing surrounding learning and teaching disciplinary knowledge and the bottlenecks that may ensue.

The Decoding Interviews: Modeling the Process of Phenomenology

The use of phenomenology as a lens for inquiry provides a starting point for interpretation of disciplinary knowledge. The interviews use open-ended questions to unpack and reveal a faculty member's own thoughts around a disciplinary bottleneck they are encountering with their students. In our study, some bottlenecks were cognitive, but others were epistemological and ontological (Miller-Young and Boman, Chapter 2). The initial interview questions were taken from the Decoding the Disciplines work by Pace and Middendorf (2004). Questions emerged during the interview process but usually started with: "Tell me about your bottleneck?" Typically Decoding uses cognitive probes to uncover tacit knowledge such as: How did you know? How did you acquire this knowledge yourself in order to teach it? How would you do that kind of thinking? How do you know when you have got it? We also used interview questions surrounding pictures, models, and metaphors such as: What does this knowledge look like to you? Can you describe it for me in a picture or metaphor? (Pace and Middendorf 2004). However, our interview questions evolved over time as the FLC noticed that faculty often drew on experiences to describe their bottlenecks, particularly when they were having trouble articulating their thinking process. This led intuitively to asking more phenomenological questions of inquiry that involved the sensory perception of experiencing the phenomena: "How did you get the sense that you know this? How have you personally experienced this knowledge? What is it about this lived experience that speaks to you? What does it feel like when you have got it?" It is interesting to note that with noncognitive bottlenecks identified by faculty, interviewers began to use a line of questioning involving more experiences of the body, but even in very cognitive bottlenecks (such as the engineering example I describe later) an embodied sense of the concept was revealed.

Initially the Decoding questions could be baffling and overwhelming to answer. Faculty described a sense of frustration at having to explain themselves in explicit terms. As Bonnie stated when asked how she knew which story idea to pursue for a journalism story: "Yeah, ... like how is it that I just know?? I just KNOW." She goes on to describe that the disciplinary knowledge is part of the journalism profession and has been passed down to others, but it remains tacit knowledge as it is not verbalized or written down explicitly but comes through exposure to experiencing the disciplinary phenomena firsthand.

During the interviews, faculty also described when they personally became more conscious of disciplinary phenomena, which are aligned with phenomenology. Colin, a professor of drama, became more conscious of his discipline when he described helping his students learn the art of conveying human emotions on the stage and realized: "That is one of the biggest things I do [with my students], I expand the attention." This is inherently phenomenological. As Smith (2013) writes,

> much of our intentional mental activity is not conscious at all, but may become conscious in the process of therapy or interrogation, as we come to realize how we feel or think about something. We should allow, then, that the

domain of phenomenology—our own experience—spreads out from conscious experience into semi-conscious and even unconscious mental activity, along with relevant background conditions implicitly invoked in our experience. (3)

The phenomenological perspective enabled me to see how the Decoding questions evolved over time as interviewers and faculty became more conscious of phenomena and the sensory experiences that were revealed during the interviews.

Ways of Practicing and Disciplinary Knowledge

As the FLC conducted the Decoding interviews we heard faculty addressing the question of how they came to know their discipline and what it meant to them. We categorized these responses as "ways of practicing" (Entwistle 2005), which is how we acquire knowledge about our disciplines as we work within them and describes a dynamic relationship between the self and the discipline through practice. Van Manen (2014) describes a phenomenology of practice as the "practice of living, as opening up possibilities for creative formative relations between being and acting, between who we are and how we act, between thoughtfulness and tact" (69–70). Within the Decoding interviews and in thinking about disciplinary knowledge, faculty members described living the experience of the discipline as practitioners or people within the practice and not thinking about what they were learning while in the moment experiencing the phenomena. Through the interviews faculty began to describe how their experience helped them understand disciplinary knowledge. This understanding is reflected in Louisa's comments as she described how she has come to know nursing, "I have seen it and I learned from experience, I learned from practice and, I guess, you know, you learn from examples, either from your own practice or from watching others and how they have dealt with things." This idea aligns with phenomenology as knowledge is achieved through the nature of consciousness and increased awareness, or an ontological or subjective perspective (Smith 2013). The inquiry into this conscious experience entails description and interpretation of the living sense of the experience. It is through interpretation (visible in the Decoding interviews) that we give expression to this experience. As the lived experience is deconstructed and unpacked, phenomenology tries to make explicit the structures of meaning in the lived experience (Van Manen 2014, 11). Lived experience becomes the starting point for understanding the phenomenon of interest. As Merleau- Ponty writes: "The world is not what I think, but what I live through" (1945, xvi–xvii).

The faculty members were able to recount what they had learned from their ways of practicing over time in their disciplines. Their experiences are congruent with phenomenological inquiry where new meanings may

NEW DIRECTIONS FOR TEACHING AND LEARNING • DOI: 10.1002/tl

emerge about phenomena that draws "something forgotten into visibility" (Harman 2007, 92). Juan Carlos, a journalism professor, stated how he has come to know journalism and his place within it: "I am conscious of voice in journalism...I am conscious of the machinery and the process by which the journalism is produced, and I have seen it all from the inside and so I know what it is, and that is where a true critique of any piece of writing, I think, has to start, with an understanding of the conditions of production of it—of that piece." Wendy, a nursing professor, discussed how nursing was a science and an art, and she expressed how she now had the perspective that the art of nursing was learned while doing nursing. It became part of her lived experience of being a nurse and was now part of her way of practicing:

> I developed that myself; I had some of it but I had to develop it, and I continue to develop it. So maybe that is part of the art of conversation, or the art of asking those bigger questions, and the art of seeing that as the role of the nurse...So not just conceptually we talk about it, but also how are you going to do this with, your patients or the family so they get more comfortable with that?

Louisa highlighted how she cannot turn off the disciplinary knowledge of performing a nursing assessment and continues her ways of practicing in everyday activities of daily living: "I walk down the street and I see people with large abdomens and I am thinking, 'You have heart failure or liver failure,' right? ... I see people with grey skin and I am thinking, 'You need to stop drinking. You need to stop smoking.' Like these are things... you are always assessing." As we explored the "ways of practicing," faculty members intuitively described the process of what phenomenologists call the "prereflective." This idea is described next.

Prereflective Practice

Phenomenologists assert that, to be aware of what is around us, we must bring things into our consciousness (Van Manen 1990). This act of becoming conscious is part of what Heidegger framed as "Being-in-the-world" or human everyday existence (Annells 1996, 706). When we become more conscious of phenomena, we become more embodied in the world and according to Van Manen (1990), our bodies become more infused with consciousness. We relate more to the world as we wonder and interpret things, processes, and activities.

We must distinguish the pre phenomenal being of experience which involves according to Husserl (1991) experiencing everyday phenomena in the first person or subjective point of view. When we turn toward these experiences in reflection and assign a quality of "mineness" to the experience, we become aware of them as phenomena (Gallagher and Zahari 2014).

New Directions for Teaching and Learning • DOI: 10.1002/tl

As Husserl (1991) said,

> When we turn toward the experience attentively and grasp it, it takes on a new mode of being: it becomes "differentiated," "singled out." And this differentiating is precisely nothing other than the grasping; and the differentiatedness is being-grasped, being the object of our turning-towards. (132)

Phenomenological inquiry helps us to gain insights into how we experience the world prereflectively and how we view and interact with our everydayness. Prereflection is about seeing phenomena in a new light, not relying on our previous ways of categorizing experience. "In order to see the world and grasp it as paradoxical, we must break with our familiar acceptance of it." (Merleau-Ponty 1945, xiv).

This idea of being prereflective and not categorizing phenomena when they are experienced emerged in one of the journalism interviews. Bonnie spoke about the idea of allowing herself to fully experience her story ideas with a fresh perspective. She stated: "I am really friendly with all my story ideas, like I just really respect them and think 'yeah, this could be, this could be'... so I am very friendly with them ... things don't pop into my head that I immediately reject as stupid or not worth pursuing."

A phenomenological inquiry explores what is given in moments of prereflective, prepredicative experience—experiences as we live through them (Van Manen 2014, 27). The Decoding interviews provided insights into the experience of "knowing the discipline" in this kind of prereflective way, in a way that intertwines reflection and experience in an immediate sense. Colin, the drama professor, highlighted that he reads a play upward of 60 times in order to make the nuances and complexities of the work more conscious and as a way to rediscover first experience. He asked himself six questions, which I align with prereflective practice and the art of turning toward an experience to single it out:

> There are ... five questions, yeah—that you have to use to sort of explore and give them circumstance around, like "Who am I? Where am I? When am I?" and "Why am I?" meaning what is the context of events and histories that have led me to this exact moment. "For what purpose am I?" so for what am I trying to achieve and what is my purpose within this? And then there is a sixth question that you start doing around the end, "What am I doing?"

In this sense he draws himself back to the present moment of practice.

The Decoding interviews revealed how faculty described and interpreted how they came to know their disciplines in deeply experiential ways. This experiential knowing was often an "embodied knowing," which is discussed next.

Embodied Knowing

The interviews demonstrated how each faculty member's disciplinary knowledge was experienced firsthand. Merleau-Ponty (1945), in *The Phenomenology of Perception*, explores experiencing phenomena with the body. The spatiality of the body is understood as the role of environment and space in which one lives and works, and the connectedness of the body to the world is recognized within the concept of temporality, as opposed to linear time. The lived body is seen as a physical being within the concept of corporality, and the body as it exists in relation to others is relationality (Annells 1996; Smith 2013; Van Manen 1990). Merleau-Ponty captures his embodied, existential form of phenomenology, with the following:

> When I reflect on the essence of subjectivity, I find it bound up with that of the body and that of the world, this is because my existence as subjectivity [= consciousness] is merely one with my existence as a body and with the existence of the world, and because the subject that I am, when taken concretely, is inseparable from this body and this world. (1945, 475)

For Merleau-Ponty, the body is considered the primary site of knowing the world, and the body and what it perceives cannot be separated from each other (Havi 2008). This perceptual experience of becoming aware of something through the senses can take the tangible form of an idea, quality, or feeling. As Merleau-Ponty said, "In perception we do not think the object and we do not think ourselves thinking it, we are given over to the object and we merge into this body which is better informed than we are about the world" (1945, 277).

The Decoding interviews uncovered how faculty came to know and understand disciplinary knowledge. In many cases, the experience of coming to know these phenomena was similar to Merleau-Ponty's (1945) expression of embodiment. Faculty described experiencing these disciplinary concepts as not being separate from themselves but a part of their bodily experience. This idea is particularly evident in how Patricia responded to the question about whether she gets cues from the physical relationship to the world in which she is moving:

> Yeah, I guess, I know it without thinking about it, probably ... as a car is accelerating forward we talk about the forces between the wheels and the ground, and usually we compare it to walking. If you are trying to accelerate forwards then you have to push backwards on the ground to move, and it is the ground that is pushing back and pushing you forwards, so it is the same thing for a car's wheels.

Patricia described the bodily experience of the ground pushing back on her within the process of walking in order to describe for students the forces at work in physics. This experience is an inherently phenomenological sense of the world. As well when asked to explain her awareness of her body feeling heavier or lighter in an elevator when it is accelerating or decelerating, Patricia explained:

> When you first start moving up in an elevator you feel heavier because there is that total force underneath you which has to be higher than your weight to start moving you and accelerating you upwards. When you start going down in the elevator you feel light for a second when it is accelerating down because that force underneath you is actually lighter than your weight while the elevator is accelerating.

Faculty members essentially described experiencing noncognitive and corporeal experiences of everyday practices when asked how they had come to know disciplinary knowledge. Colin, the drama professor, described directing his students to feel their bodies to get in touch with specific physical senses (corporality). "So the next time you do this I want you to make sure you are ... I want you to focus on your knees being like rubber as you move through it, ... and then seeing what happens and then letting them [students] reflect back on what happens as a result of that." This example illustrates experiencing knowledge through the senses.

Van Manen (1997) goes further when discussing embodied knowing and states that professional knowledge is often tied to pathic knowledge, which is the "sense and sensuality of the body, personal presence, relational perceptiveness, tact for knowing what to say and do in contingent situations, thoughtful routines and practices, and other aspects of knowledge that are in part prereflective, pre-theoretic, pre-linguistic" (20). He goes on to say that pathic knowledge is a "felt sense of being in the world" (21). "Pathic knowledge expresses itself in the confidence with which we do things, the way that we 'feel,' the atmosphere of a place, the manner in which we can 'read' someone's face, and so forth" (21). Colin described perceiving just this kind of pathic knowledge when he feels a sense of tangible resistance in the room when students were not in touch with the character they were portraying. "There is resistance there, and so then I have to discover who brought resistance and why is it there in the room with us? So it is those sorts of cues that I look for, and part of it is that I base it on years of ... so, like, I spent twenty plus years directing professionally in Canada so there is a feeling when things are cooking and I can point to lots of clues." Bonnie, a professor of journalism, discusses the elements of a great story and she describes her bodily response to a great idea by physically feeling a sense of tension: "Well I guess I identify tension ... by being able to recognize discourse, disharmony; ... I guess I actually identify tension by what it is I feel in response to the idea."

Merleau-Ponty (1945) describes the sensory experience of being in the world with the following: "We do not say that the notion of the world is inseparable from that of the subject. Or that the subject thinks himself inseparable from the idea of his body and the idea of the world" (474–475). Faculty members did not realize that they had internalized the concepts within their disciplines over time and as part of their practice, and they became increasingly aware of how they had done so through the Decoding interview process. These disciplinary concepts had essentially become part of their being. They embodied them as they lived through the experience of gaining this knowledge and found it difficult to understand how students struggle with coming to know and understand this same knowledge. Van Manen (1997) describes that lived space as "felt" space and that we become the space we are in (102). In other words, disciplinary experts are not able to separate themselves from the experience; they become part of it. This then could lead to the development of more bottlenecks that students find difficult to navigate because they have not personally experienced the concepts in a lived way.

Analysis of the Decoding interviews using phenomenology has extended Pace and Middendorf's work (2004) and reveals that, even for cognitive bottlenecks, expert thinking is not just a cognitive process but involves living the experience of the discipline, bringing disciplinary knowledge into consciousness, and bringing forth the embodied experience of knowing to help faculty members to understand why their students may be experiencing bottlenecks.

Implications for Educators

How does an understanding of the Decoding the Disciplines from a phenomenological perspective inform the teaching process? The implications for educators are significant and are discussed next.

Living the Experience.   The interviews revealed that one needs to live the experience in order to fully embody the disciplinary concepts. This idea was a common thread throughout all the interviews and involves taking the time of living through the experience. When Wendy was asked about how she knew what is important in nursing, she responded with the following:

> Well I think just from doing it for years, and years and years and doing it
> …sometimes with a community, sometimes with a family, sometimes with
> a bigger population when I have developed or worked with…I could see it
> firsthand when I was working with people in their homes, right, and in the
> school setting. So I could see things that were influencing their health and
> that what they were struggling with was much bigger.

Thus, living the experience supports the importance of exposure to the everydayness of clinical practice and working through experiences in the world in clinical practicums, simulations, and laboratory experiences for practice disciplines. As Wendy said: "so certainly exposure to community and exposure to those settings helped me to understand it." Interviewees said they came away with a larger understanding of how the significant years of experience influenced their understanding of concepts within their discipline. For educators who see students struggling with a particular bottleneck, they might consider reflecting on how they came to know what they know, what they were personally exposed to within their disciplinary experience, and sharing these insights with students. Bonnie, the journalism professor, had been reluctant to share her lived experience with her students. However, near the end of the Decoding process she came to this realization of the value of sharing her lived experience as "story":

> and yet as I talk to you, you asked a lot about, "How would I do this" and "what would that look like?" and if done the right way maybe be my students could benefit from me making those steps, a little clearer, and maybe enabling them to ask not only of me, but of other more experienced journalists in the discipline the kind of questions that exposes the "how to" part.

Developing Embodied Knowing.   The interviews illustrated that faculty had often learned the complexities and nuances within their disciplines over years and sometimes with a sensory response from their bodies. As educators we need to help students to pay attention to the noncognitve reactions they experience in learning our disciplines; the acquisition of embodied knowledge and pathic knowledge. We need to call attention with our students to our bodies and the experiential experiences in the laboratory and simulation settings and the real world. Bourdieu, a sociologist studying the theory of practice, describes the physical sensations experienced with simple social commands that can be shared with students as examples of the body entangled with the world:

> Nothing seems more ineffable, more incommunicable, more inimitable, and, therefore, more precious, than the values given body, made body by the transubstantiation achieved by the hidden persuasion of an implicit pedagogy, capable of instilling a whole cosmology, an ethic, a metaphysic, a political philosophy, through injunctions as insignificant as "stand up straight" or "don"t hold your knife in your left hand." (1977, 94)

Within practice disciplines where we experience the world with types of knowledge related to touch, perceptions, feelings, actions, and sensations that cannot necessarily be translated or captured in conceptualizations and theoretical representations, we need to give them expression and importance. It is our interactions with the world and our bodies that places us in the world (Merleau-Ponty 1945, xvi).

Implications for Decoders.   The Decoding questions helped faculty members to break down the disciplinary knowledge, to make the connections, and to make the acquisition of knowledge more conscious. The questions pushed the faculty to have to articulate and put into language what was difficult to articulate: How do you know? This study has shown that asking about sensory perceptions of phenomena should be included in the Decoding the Discipline process. If we were to conduct this study again, we might ask interviewees "What happens to you personally when you read the Code of Ethics? What do you feel like when you are thinking about the dimensions of walking? What is the essence of this news story and what does that feel like? How do you make your relationship to this story, this play dynamic for your students?" Future Decoding work could assess how ways of thinking and practicing could be further revealed with questioning along these lines.

Conclusion

Philosophers within the phenomenological approach look at who they are in relation to others, considering multiple realities to understand the full context of their own experience. They consider how they relate to this experience through the embodiment of practice and are curious to know more about their situation in the world. Similarly, the Decoding the Disciplines process reveals how we come to understand disciplinary knowledge. Our interview process, intuitively developed as we struggled with decoding complex disciplinary knowledge, unpacked the phenomena faculty have learned through "living the experience" and made it conscious. Faculty members gave voice to how they practice and put a language to the experience. Their responses helped us recognize the embodied, experiential sense of their ways of practicing, and opens new avenues for exploring the use of Decoding using experiential and sensory questions.

Acknowledgment

I would like to thank Michelle Yeo for sharing her knowledge of phenomenology and her encouraging feedback on earlier drafts of this paper.

References

Annells, Merilyn. 1996. "Hermeneutic Phenomenology: Philosophical Perspectives and Current Use in Nursing Research." *Journal of Advanced Nursing* 23: 705–713.

Bourdieu, Pierre. 1977. *Outline of a Theory of Practice*. Cambridge: Cambridge University Press.

Entwistle, Noel. 2005. "Learning Outcomes and Ways of Thinking Across Contrasting Disciplines and Settings in Higher Education." *Curriculum Journal* 16 (1): 67–82.

Gallagher, Shaun and Zahavi, Dan, "Phenomenological Approaches to Self-Consciousness", *The Stanford Encyclopedia of Philosophy* (Winter 2016 Edition), Edward N. Zalta (ed.), Retrieved on April 3, 2017 from https://plato.stanford.edu/archives/win2016/entries/self-consciousness-phenomenological/.

Harman, Graham. 2007. *Heidegger Explained: From Phenomenon to Thing*. Illinois: Open Court.

Havi, Carel. 2008. *Illness: The Cry of the Flesh*. Stocksfield, UK: Acumen.

Husserl, Edmund. 1991. *On the Phenomenology of the Consciousness of Internal Time (1893–1917)*. Dordrecht. The Netherlands: Kluwer.

Laverty, Susann. 2003. "Hermeneutic Phenomenology and Phenomenology: A Comparison of Historical and Methodological Considerations." *International Journal of Qualitative Methods* 2 (3): 1–29.

Merleau-Ponty, Merleau. 1945. *The Phenomenology of Perception*. London: Routledge and Kegan Paul.

Pace, David, and Joan Middendorf, eds. 2004. *New Directions for Teaching and Learning: No. 98. Decoding the Disciplines: Helping Students Learn Disciplinary Ways of Thinking*. San Francisco: Jossey-Bass.

Polkingthorne, Donald. 1983. *Methodology for the Human Sciences: Systems of Inquiry*. Albany: State University of New York Press.

Rilke, Ranier Maria. 1987. *Rilke and Benvenuta: An Intimate Correspondence*. New York: Fromm International.

Smith, David Woodruff. 2013. *Phenomenology: The Stanford Encyclopedia of Philosophy*, edited by Edward N. Zalta. http://plato.stanford.edu/archives/win2013/entries/phenomenology/

Van Manen, Max. 1990. *Researching Lived Experience: Human Science for an Action Sensitive Pedagogy*. London, Ontario: University of Western Ontario.

Van Manen, Max. 1997. "Phenomenology of Practice." *Phenomenology and Practice* 1 (1): 11—30.

Van Manen, Max. 2014. *Phenomenology of Practice: Meaning Giving Methods in Phenomenological Research and Writing*. Walnut Creek, CA: Left Coast Press.

Van der Zalm, Jeanne, and Vangie Bergum. 2000. "Hermeneutic Phenomenology: Providing Living Knowledge for Nursing Practice." *Journal of Advanced Nursing* 31 (1), 211–218.

GENEVIEVE CURRIE *has been a faculty member at Mount Royal University since 2001 and teaches in the School of Nursing and Midwifery.*

NEW DIRECTIONS FOR TEACHING AND LEARNING • DOI: 10.1002/tl

This chapter argues that expert practice is an inquiry that surfaces a hermeneutic relationship between theory, practice, and the world, with implications for new lines of questioning in the Decoding interview.

Decoding the Disciplines as a Hermeneutic Practice

Michelle Yeo

Insight is more than the knowledge of this or that situation. It always involves an escape from something that had deceived us and held us captive. Thus insight always involves an element of self-knowledge and constitutes a necessary side of what we called experience in the proper sense. Insight is something we come to.

Gadamer (1999, 356)

Introduction

Decoding the disciplines is an approach with fundamentally cognitivist assumptions. Bottlenecks, which are areas of the discipline where students can get "stuck" or "interrupted" in their learning (Middendorf and Pace 2004, 4–5), are typically described in conceptual terms, and the Decoding process was originally designed to help experts unpack their own cognitive processes. Using the Decoding interview technique (Pace and Middendorf 2004), experts are guided to unpack troublesome areas for students, working through how they approach and "think through" such difficulties as experts. However, in our interviews of seven faculty members from four diverse disciplines as described in Chapter 2 of this issue, we observed that many of the bottlenecks described had more to do with ways of being-in-the-world, having affective, relational, and identity elements. As others have argued for the scholarship of teaching and learning (SoTL) more broadly (Miller-Young and Yeo 2015; Poole 2013), we suggest that taking an interpretive rather than a strictly cognitive approach (as shown through several, if not all of the other chapters in this special issue) would enrich the

NEW DIRECTIONS FOR TEACHING AND LEARNING, no. 150, Summer 2017 © 2017 Wiley Periodicals, Inc.
Published online in Wiley Online Library (wileyonlinelibrary.com) • DOI: 10.1002/tl.20237

possibilities inherent in Decoding work. In this analysis, a hermeneutic approach is undertaken as a lens with which to unpack disciplinary elements related to openness to questions, the interpretation of experience, the nature of knowledge, our relationship to language and text, and being-in-the-world. A hermeneutic philosophy has much to say about all of these elements we found present in the interviews, and thus a hermeneutic reading can help to enrich our understanding of the Decoding process.

Hermeneutics

It will not be possible within the scope of this chapter to outline the whole of hermeneutics. However, I highlight certain key elements in order to set the stage for the analysis. The approach taken for this analysis is to focus on the aspects of the interviews that surfaced powerful hermeneutic elements.

Hermeneutics, at its heart, is about interpretation. It argues for the "basic interpretability of life itself" (Smith 1991, 199). Interpretive methodologies recognize our own situatedness within the topic of the inquiry, a kind of inhabitation of the questions. This idea becomes relevant to this set of interviews, because each demonstrates a living into the discipline through deeply tacit knowledge. The interview itself becomes a disruption to the tacit, where the familiar becomes strange. Mayers (2001) writes of hermeneutics, "Understanding and interpretation come from a tension that lives in between what is familiar to us and what is unfamiliar" (6). Hermeneutics is a tradition with a long history, usually traced beginning with Schleiermacher and Husserl and further developed through the work of Heidegger and Gadamer. It is largely a Gadamerian conception of hermeneutics from which I draw for the purposes of this analysis. Moran (2002) describes Gadamer's approach thus:

> Hermeneutics is the art of interpretation or understanding, and, for Gadamer, always signifies an ongoing, never completable process of understanding, rooted in human finitude and human linguisticality. Gadamer follows Heidegger's Being and Time in seeing understanding as the central manner of human being-in-the-world. Humans are essentially involved in the historically situated and finite task of understanding the world, a world encountered and inhabited in and through language.... Philosophy, then, is a conversation leading towards mutual understanding, a conversation, furthermore, where this very understanding comes as something genuinely experienced. (248–249)

Gadamer (1999) sees this experience of understanding as a profoundly linguistic event, with the relationship between texts (broadly defined) and our lives, and additionally, between the old and the new. Not only does the text have something to say about the decision we make today or the way we read or understand a situation, but this new situation then helps us recast

NEW DIRECTIONS FOR TEACHING AND LEARNING • DOI: 10.1002/tl

the past and see the text anew. Gadamer writes, "So also it is universally true of texts that only in the process of understanding them is the dead trace of meaning transformed back into living meaning" (164). This is known as the "hermeneutic circle." Thus, a particular understanding of experience is invoked. Experience becomes interpretable and a way of making meaning.

In the following, I explore the hermeneutic conceptions of openness to questions, the relationship to text, and the nature of knowledge and experience. The Decoding interview itself can be read as a hermeneutic task, as the interviewer attempts to achieve deep understanding of the discipline through the play of question and answer. Gadamer (1999) in describing dialogue, might indeed have been speaking of the Decoding process:

> To conduct a conversation means to allow oneself to be conducted by the subject matter to which the partners in the dialogue are oriented. It requires that one does not try to argue the other person down but that one really considers the weight of the other's opinion. Hence it is an art of testing. But the art of testing is the art of questioning. For we have seen that to question means to lay open, to place in the open. As against the fixity of opinions, questioning makes the object and all its possibilities fluid. (367)

Gadamer argues that questioning "is more a passion than an action. A question presses itself on us, we can no longer avoid it and persist in our accustomed opinion" (366). As a result of the dialogic process of analyzing the Decoding interviews, what follows is a surfacing of the hermeneutic concepts deeply present in the interviewees' descriptions of their work within their disciplines, revealing hermeneutic structures within the disciplines themselves.

Openness to Questions

> Be patient toward all that is unsolved in your heart and try to love the questions themselves.
>
> Rilke (1993, Letter Four)

Gadamer (1999) demonstrates a particular orientation to ideas, framed as questions that "breach" or break open a conversation in a new way. He writes:

> Such ideas do not occur to us entirely unexpectedly. They always presuppose an orientation toward an area of openness from which the idea can occur— i.e. they presuppose questions. The real nature of the sudden idea is perhaps less that a solution occurs to us like an answer to a riddle than that a question occurs to us that breaks through into the open and thereby makes an answer

possible. Hence we say that a question too "occurs" to us, that it "arises" or "presents itself" more than that we raise it or present it. (366)

Such an orientation was present most strikingly in Bonnie's interview. Bonnie described how stories address an experienced journalist. In a way that echoes Gadamer, she talks about the way in which a good story creates a breach, how it "breaks through into the open and thereby makes an answer possible" (Gadamer 1999, 366). She told us, "[It is] those unexplored angles and when you pull them up to the surface they are typically like, tension laden. Tension laden." When asked how she knows when something exhibits tension, she explained,

Well I guess I identify tension... by being able to recognize discord, disharmony; I identify tension by what it is that I feel in response to the idea.... Like when there is a good idea and there is tension I emotionally engage with that idea, as a producer, as a faculty member, as a journalist I can just emotionally engage with that idea quickly.

Interviewer: And what does that engagement look like?

[Pause] ... I don't know! ... well I mean on a first level it is just excitement, I am excited by the idea. I am kind of excited by the notion of, "A-ha! There is something here we are going to bring out, that we are going to surface that has never potentially not been surfaced before," so that idea, the big reveal.

A central tenet of Gadamer's hermeneutics is dialogic, but dialogic for the purposes of coming to understanding. In his analysis of the earlier philosophy of Schleiermacher Gadamer (1999) comments, "The 'method' of understanding will be concerned equally with what is common, by comparison, and with what is unique, by intuition" (190). An intuitive sense of what is unique, and therefore, a story worth telling, is what Bonnie has developed as an experienced journalist. In part, this is done by maintaining her natural curiosity, combined with continuous and astute consumption of media.

Bonnie speaks of the importance of being friendly to ideas, almost as though she is engaging in a dialogic process with the story itself. She explained:

I am really friendly with all my story ideas like I just really respect them... and think yeah, this could be, this could be, and then when I am in a story meeting I do enough preliminary research to kind of back my claim of a story idea with at least some evidence so that by the time it gets to the story idea nobody rejects it... things don't pop in my head that I immediately reject as stupid or not worth pursuing.

New Directions for Teaching and Learning • DOI: 10.1002/tl

This echoes Gadamer's notion that at the heart of hermeneutic dialogue is the possibility that the other person might be right. In this case, it is the story itself that emerges and has the potential to teach us something.

Bonnie's interview also contained sensitivity to generativity, complexity, and resisting the reduction of narratives to simple binaries, all inherently hermeneutic. A sense of openness to questions is also seen in Colin's interview. When speaking about how he approaches scripts, he used exactly the same phrase as Bonnie: "I have to keep myself open to what else could be." His discipline is theatre, and his perspective slips between director, teacher, and consultant in the business community on creativity and play. It is his interview I will now explore more fully.

Relationship to Text

> The hermeneutic consciousness seeks to confront that will with something of the truth of remembrance: with what is still and ever again real.
>
> Gadamer (1999, xxxviii)

Colin's interview beautifully laid out a hermeneutic understanding of the relationship to text. He told us in his interview that he reads a script fifty or sixty times before starting rehearsal, and although the text itself is necessarily static on the page there is always the possibility of discovering something new:

> What usually happens is that … I will start reading it … I do it not because I want to, or because I enjoy it but because I know I have to. I will start reading through it and it will just be like I am going through the same story again and it tells me something, but then all of a sudden I will notice something in this story or script, or a character and their relationship to another character that had never before been apparent or had caught my attention, and so that one piece of information can sometimes be a key to an entire scene. I am always amazed, like, "How could I have read it so many times and never got that?"

We thus can see how our reading, interpretation, and experience of a text then becomes dynamic rather than static. The text itself has not changed, but with a deep inhabitation of fifty readings, we discover something new, which then changes our understanding of the text as a whole and how we live into it. Gadamer (1999) writes, "A written tradition, once deciphered and read, is to such an extent pure mind that it speaks to us as if in the present. That is why the capacity to read, to understand what is written, is like a secret art, even a magic that frees and binds us" (163). This capacity for the creation of something living out of static text is deeply woven into the performing arts. Indeed, Gadamer uses the notion of performance, whether of theatre or ritual, to explain the hermeneutic circle:

From its inception—whether instituted in a single act or introduced gradually—the nature of a festival is to be celebrated regularly. Thus its own original essence is always to be something different (even when celebrated in exactly the same way). An entity that exists only by always being something different is temporal in a more radical sense than everything that belongs to history. It has its being only in becoming and return. (123)

Colin describes a kind of intersubjective inhabitation he engages in with the actors.

So in rehearsals you would start to then see what happens, like as you bring the actor closer to the information you see what happens when people are actually moving within a physical environment that resembles the place in which they occupy, and then bringing into play their imagination, bringing to mind sense, experience and memory and seeing what sense, experience and memory comes as you move inside of this physical place, given this information and moving it towards you.... Space holds memory.

Colin here echoes Gadamer (1999), when he notes, "Play is more than the consciousness of the player, and so it is more than a subjective act. Language is more than the consciousness of the speaker; so also it is more than a subjective act" (xxxvi). Juan Carlos, in journalism, spoke to the notion that we are "always already" in the world and that language is indeed part of our ways of knowing. He explained:

The problem is that objectivity in any pure sense, in any sense of mimicking reality is impossible for any number of reasons. The first is that journalists are already, in some situation, or some situatedness and they can't escape that, and also language, which as a social construct cannot mimic reality.

Or in Gadamer's (1999) terms, "The conceptual world in which philosophizing develops has already captivated us in the same way that the language in which we live conditions us" (xxv). Gadamer further explains his interest, "My real concern was and is philosophic: not what we do or what we ought to do, but what happens to us over and above our wanting and doing" (xxviii). There is a deep sense in which all three of the participants mentioned thus far, Bonnie, Colin, and Juan Carlos, are interested similarly in having their students delve into the depths of what happens to us "over and above our wanting and doing." They don't want their students to become objective—all three of these participants do not believe in an objective stance, but rather, they desire their students to step back from the constructed narratives to deeper questions of interpretation and meaning. As Colin expressed, "There is a line in theatre which is, 'Character is situation,' and in a way who you are exists only in relation to other things and we don't exist outside of anything."

NEW DIRECTIONS FOR TEACHING AND LEARNING • DOI: 10.1002/tl

The act of hermeneutic interpretation, then, begins to hold an ethical dimension. Monique, in nursing, brings forward a final example of how the interpretation of a text must become a living interpretation with an ethical dimension; she describes a bottleneck "surrounding this idea of a document—which is the code of ethics we have in nursing – in relation to how students actually understand it in their practice." She goes on to explore the difficulty of living the code of ethics in practice, the complexity of the dilemmas nurses face that challenge their own preunderstandings (in Gadamerian terms). She explained, "I am expecting them to really live the code of ethics, I guess . . . I am, and maybe that is too much to expect." When probed by the interviewer what that might look like, she clarified, "Actually looking at the dilemma they are faced with and actually looking at different sides of it . . . so more than just being respectful." She wanted them not just to make a judgment but to actually place themselves in another's shoes with a deep kind of empathy, back to Gadamer's (1999) notion of understanding "as something genuinely *experienced*" (249). This experience is a kind of opening to the world and to the other: "the way we experience one another, the way we experience historical traditions, the way we experience the natural givenness of our existence and of our world, constitute a truly hermeneutic universe, in which we are not imprisoned, as if behind insurmountable barriers, but to which we are opened" (xxiv).

Relationship to Knowledge and Experience

> The hermeneutic phenomenon is basically not a problem of method at all. It is not concerned with a method of understanding by means of which texts are subjected to scientific investigation like all other objects of experience. It is not concerned primarily with amassing verified knowledge, such as would satisfy the methodological ideal of science—yet it too is concerned with knowledge and with truth. In understanding tradition not only are texts understood, but insights are acquired and truths known. But what kind of knowledge and what kind of truth? (Gadamer 1999, xxi)

Questions of knowledge and truth were part of each interview in different ways. Juan Carlos expresses the relationship of journalism to truth in a way that directly echoes Gadamer's perspective: "They practice journalism as though there is, as though there is a real world out there they can represent hermetically, that they can in language and in their stories capture 'the real' or 'the truth.'" The interviews demonstrate a strikingly hermeneutic expression of the expert's relationship to knowledge, which is a dynamic to-and-fro between whole and part, provisionality, and theory to practice.

Relationship of Whole and Part.   Five of the interviews explored directly the relationship of whole and part, or as framed in Chapter 2 of this issue, deconstructing and reconstructing. This chapter further explores three interviews using a hermeneutic lens. Gadamer (1999) explains that hermeneutics evolved from interpreting texts only in relation to themselves to incorporating the context which surrounds them: "The old interpretive principle of understanding the part in terms of the whole was no longer bound and limited to the dogmatic unity of the canon; it was concerned with the totality of the historical reality to which each individual historical document belonged" (177).

In Colin's descriptions of how he works with a script, he remarked on how he attends to multiple pieces that ultimately feed into the whole. He described, "There are ways in which I highlight the script and particular pieces of information—types of information—and things that are about, you know, indications of time, indications of space, indications of the psychological make-up." This ultimately feeds into the whole, but that whole is influenced not just by what is in the script and his interpretation but the gestalt of the dynamic between himself, the actors, the script, and the space. He explained how the novice finds this more difficult: "It is actually quite easy to show people how to take something apart; it is more difficult for them to understand, or then grasp after they have pulled something apart that it then all relates back together, because they become so interested in each piece individually." Similarly, Louisa in nursing described thinking about illness on multiple levels of complexity simultaneously: cellular, tissue, organ, and organ system level. She explained,

> When you are thinking about all the different modalities and how we look at different ways of approaching an alteration in health and we want everything to build on each other and so you don't willy-nilly choose a treatment, you want the treatments to build on each other and have sort of a synergistic effect . . . you want to think about the person on an organ level, but you also have to think about the many things that could be causing what you see in a patient in terms of signs and symptoms, and that might mean you need to address it in more than one way.

In a second scientific example, in Patricia's interview from the field of engineering the relationship of part to whole was specifically explored. She explained how when thinking about a dynamic physics problem:

> The idea of free body in physics or engineering is we would take the object that we are analyzing and separate it out from all of its contexts so we can just look at the one object. But to make that free body an equivalent body to what it is in context we replace everything else with forces . . . The idea of making them draw this is to help them remember that no, the tension isn't equal to the weight anymore because we have this thing on the other side that is affecting the forces, but they always seem to revert back . . . The more complex the problem they just skip over that step and just don't seem to remember to do it.

When asked later if she herself visualizes the whole, she explains, "I guess I don't try to visualize the system first because I know the more complex it is you can't just actually look at it and necessarily figure it out, and that is why it is important to look at all the pieces." Inherent in Patricia's exploration was a sense that the whole was greater than the sum of the parts. One had to understand the context, i.e., that the problem was situated as a dynamic system, rather than a static one. This then changes the "rules" of how they were to interpret the problem.

Provisionality.   Important in Patricia's descriptions, as explored by Miller-Young and Boman in Chapter 2 is the expert's ability to defer judgment, or what they call valuing provisionality. Patricia explained,

> Generally my first step would be to get a sense of well, this one is heavier so it is probably going to move down, but it also depends on a lot of complicated things that are happening over here, so I don't usually try to figure that out in advance. I try to, you know, break it down into the simple parts and look at each simple part by itself and then put it back together. When these systems get more complicated you can't actually tell just from looking at it which way it is moving.

For Gadamer, this provisionality comes into play when interpreting texts, but it has its reflection in the interviews by expert practitioners who have learned to "hold back" their own prejudices or presuppositions until they have gathered enough information. In Patricia's example, she knows she can't "tell" from just "looking" at the problem, instead she has to draw it out and let the example speak for itself. Gadamer (1999) explains this kind of process (in relation to text) thus:

> A thing does not present itself to the hermeneutical experience without an effort special to it, namely that of 'being negative toward itself.' A person who is trying to understand a text has to keep something at a distance—namely everything that suggests itself, on the basis of his own prejudices, as the meaning expected ... Explicating the whole of meaning towards which understanding is directed forces us to make interpretive conjectures and to take them back again. The self-cancellation of the interpretation makes it possible for the thing itself—the meaning of the text – to assert itself. (465)

Colin explores this provisional nature of what he terms "the super-task" in his work with actors, which is their "big picture" goal: "When I work with actors, even when we come to the super-task it is sort of a provisional super-task; it is given everything we know, this is really what it looks like, and then as we keep on working we may have to revise that." Patricia speaks of not jumping to conclusions when solving complex problems: "You have a system of equations you have to solve for the unknown, and the tension in this case might be the unknown, and you just ... you

New Directions for Teaching and Learning • DOI: 10.1002/tl

can't jump to that conclusion." She also noted that in engineering, "expert designers spend more time on the brainstorming stage thinking of lots of possibilities and evaluating those possibilities before they start developing an actual solution, whereas the novice ones, they get one idea and they go with it and are done." Monique talks about the danger of making assumptions in nursing practice, and the importance of withholding judgments based on predetermined categories:

> It is more about troubling our assumptions ... this is more about giving some-one, every person, the benefit of not making assumptions about those people. So when we are questioning assumptions we still do it in a respectful way which still aligns with the code of ethics ... It is not just about respect ... it is a capacity to think critically, with respect, with a broader view ... just a better understanding that I may not know, I maybe cannot possibly know in the situation how it is going to be, so how do I come in with an open view of this person.

Monique describes how openness and nonjudgment are in a paradoxical relation with the necessity of making decisions, which Gadamer would refer to as practical judgment, in Aristotle's terms phronesis. It echoes precisely Monique's wish that students learn not to apply the code of ethics in a mechanical way but rather internalize it while simultaneously always being open to the person standing in front of them. Gadamer (1999) explains:

> The question here, then, is not about knowledge in general but its concretion at a particular moment ... we discover that the person who is understanding does not know and judge as one who stands apart and unaffected but rather he thinks along with the other from the perspective of a specific bond of belonging, as if he too were affected. (323)

At the same time, while engaging in this deep form of empathy, one holds open the possibility that we do not really understand, especially in advance, just as Monique describes. Gadamer claims, "By understanding the other, by claiming to know him, one robs his claims of their legitimacy. In particular, the dialectic of charitable or welfare work operates in this way, penetrating all relationships ... as a reflective form of the effort to dominate" (360).

The notion of phronesis, of the practical judgment of what to do in this or that situation, leads naturally to the question of the relationship of theory and practice.

Theory to Practice.   The relationship of theory and practice surfaces most clearly in two of the nursing interviews, Louisa and Wendy's. Louisa told us of the perennial problem in professional education, the disconnection of what is learned in the classroom from the world of practice:

In this class I want the students to be able to take all the information they know around the pathophysiological process and how that manifests, in order to be able to think, "What do I need to know?" Because if they don't have an understanding of those processes, the treatment that they decide, or how they decide to go about working with their patients might not be effective, right? ... Often times students are in the dark about that because they don't have the experience to feed back on, "Well what is the point?" whereas nurses working in the field have this, "Well I see it every day, and I know ... like I took care of a patient."

This tension is an inevitable element of the educative process, particularly in professional education. It surfaced in all of the interviews: in journalism, in theatre, in engineering, and prominently in the nursing interviews. As Gadamer (1999) explains, this kind of practical knowledge demonstrates phronesis:

The old Aristotelian distinction between practical and theoretical knowledge is operative here—a distinction which cannot be reduced to that between the true and the probable. Practical knowledge, phronesis, is another kind of knowledge. Primarily, this means that it is directed towards the concrete situation. Thus it must grasp the "circumstances" in their infinite variety. (21)

The enormous complexity that Gadamer speaks of, the "infinite variety" was especially prominent in Louisa's interview. She described a process, in diagnosis and treatment, of thinking about simultaneous levels of function in the body (cellular, tissue, organ, system) and how she would cross-reference that with social factors, using the expression "*a constellation of symptoms.*" Later in her interview she described how experience with this kind of complexity, over time, would lead to a kind of "intuition" about a patient and what would happen next. As Gadamer (1999) writes, "experience teaches us to acknowledge the real" (357). Louisa also spoke in a compelling way about gathering more information, hearkening back to the idea of provisionality, and the idea that some information becomes "foreground" and other information, "background."

A lot of it is being observant and being able to say, "Ah, what else do I want to know?" I think that has really helped me in terms of understanding and gathering all the information that I need to because then you are able to prioritize and know what is foreground, know what is background ... inquire a little further around any associated symptoms a patient might be having around that.

Thus, expert practice is fundamentally an inquiry, fundamentally a hermeneutic relationship between the text, the "normal" of the body, and the infinite variety and messiness of this or that patient as presented.

NEW DIRECTIONS FOR TEACHING AND LEARNING • DOI: 10.1002/tl

Wendy, also in nursing, spoke of the importance of context:

> So for me nursing is focusing on the individual's needs, or it could be a family, it could be the community, it could be the population, because I have worked in all those areas. So I am working collaboratively, it is not my agenda, and it is working with them to find out what their agenda is and what their issues are, but it is to also consider the broader influences that have brought them to this place; so what was happening in their family of origin? What was happening in their childhood? What is happening in their environment? What is happening in their work setting? What is happening in their family support? What is happening with how they have learned to cope and their coping style and their ways of dealing with things?

A hermeneutic understanding of the world is one in which context is paramount, where a sense of historicity is integral to interpreting experience and life itself. It is not the case that one can put aside one's prejudices; rather, a hermeneutic consciousness comes to a mature awareness of their extent and their situatedness: "A person who does not admit that he is dominated by prejudices will fail to see what manifests itself by their light" (Gadamer 1999, 360–361). This then is a simultaneous recognition of one's own context and how it predisposes one to perceive others. This idea relates to the notion of provisionality: the experienced expert has learned to "hold back" their own prejudgments, but first, to be aware of them. This process is not one of eliminating historicity, but rather, as Gadamer suggests, "in human relations the important thing is, as we have seen, to experience the Thou truly as a thou—i.e., not to overlook his claim but to let him really say something to us. Here is where openness belongs" (361).

Implications

A hermeneutic approach to Decoding the Disciplines, then, has implications both for the interviewing practice of Decoding as well as for educators in the classroom. A dialogic approach to the interviews, where interviewers open a space for experts to descriptively explore and express their understandings, as Gadamer (1999) says, "to really say something to us" (361) is paramount. This approach then requires interviewers to put aside their own preconceptions and the "historicity" of their own discipline. Further, it can suggest certain avenues of questioning if a dead end is reached with cognitively framed questions or with bottlenecks that have more to do with ways of being-in-the-world. In cases where the bottleneck has to do with a living understanding of text, for example, in our interviews where Colin describes the relationship with the script or Monique explores the code of ethics, questions might be asked to further surface this relationship. Decoders might ask interviewees for living examples of how they interpret the texts they work with. As a possibility, Monique might have been asked for a specific instance of how the code of ethics manifested in her practice in a way that required critical thinking rather than mechanical implementation. Questions might also be asked to surface elements such as the experts' orientation to questions, their sense of play in their discipline, provisionality, or the historical context of their discipline.

For educators in the classroom, a hermeneutic understanding of discipline expands the repertoire far beyond information sharing. It begins to ask the teacher to conceptualize teaching within a broader framework of teaching within a discipline as communicating an epistemology and an ontology—ways of seeing, knowing, and practicing. It is not just the information itself, but rather, the information contextualized within the discipline's historically steeped relationship to the world. A hermeneutic approach also asks that educators enter into a dialogic relationship with students, and just as in the Decoding process, asks that we not "overlook the claim" (Gadamer 1999, 361) students are making in their novice understandings of the discipline. It means that we are not only focused solely on making it easier for students to understand us as teachers or to decode the content. Rather, it means that we are simultaneously focused on understanding the students better and how they are experiencing the discipline. It asks us to more deeply inquire into the nature of student confusion in a generous way, rather than merely with a view to a quick fix. It requires, in Gadamerian terms, a kind of "fundamental openness" (361). This kind of openness is, at its best, at the heart of the pedagogical relationship.

References

Gadamer, Hans-Georg. 1999. *Truth and Method*, 2nd ed. Translated by Joel Weinsheimer and Donald G. Marshall. New York: Continuum.

Mayers, Marjorie. 2001. *Street Kids and Streetscapes*. New York: Peter Lang Publishing.

Middendorf, Joan, and David Pace. 2004. "Decoding the Disciplines: A Model for Helping Students Learn Disciplinary Ways of Thinking." In *New Directions for Teaching and Learning: No. 98. Decoding the Disciplines: Helping Students Learn Disciplinary Ways of Thinking*, edited by David Pace and Joan Middendorf, 1–12. San Francisco: Jossey-Bass.

Miller-Young, Janice, and Michelle Yeo. 2015. "Conceptualizing and Communicating SoTL: A Framework for the Field." *Teaching and Learning Inquiry* 3 (2): 37–53.

Moran, Dermot. 2002. "Hans-Georg Gadamer: Philosophical Hermeneutics" In *The Phenomenology Reader*, edited by Dermot Moran and Tim Mooney, 248–286. London: Routledge.

Pace, David, and Joan Middendorf, eds. 2004. *New Directions for Teaching and Learning: No. 98. Decoding the Disciplines: Helping Students Learn Disciplinary Ways of Thinking*. San Francisco: Jossey-Bass.

Poole, Gary. 2013. "Square One: What Is Research?" In *The Scholarship of Teaching and Learning in and across the Disciplines*, edited by K. McKinney, 135–151. Bloomington: Indiana University Press.

Rilke, Rainer Maria. 1993. *Letters to a Young Poet*. Translated by M. D. Herter Norton. New York: WW Norton & Co.

Smith, David G. 1991. "Hermeneutic Inquiry: The Hermeneutic Imagination and the Pedagogic Text." In *Forms of Curriculum Inquiry*, edited by Edmund C. Short, 187–207. Albany, New York: State University of New York Press.

MICHELLE YEO has been a faculty developer and faculty member in Mount Royal University's Academic Development Centre since 2007.

NEW DIRECTIONS FOR TEACHING AND LEARNING • DOI: 10.1002/tl

5

Deciphering teachers' paths to their disciplinary professional identities can make important elements of their tacit knowledge explicit and available to their students.

Intuitions and Instincts: Considerations for Decoding Disciplinary Identities

Ron MacDonald

Interviews of teachers seeking to help students overcome learning bottle-necks are the first steps in a process of Decoding the Disciplines (Pace and Middendorf 2004) pioneered in the history department at Indiana University. The aim of a Decoding interview is to build precise understanding of the bottleneck in question and to identify the operations or steps experts would take and students must master to get through the bottleneck. Teach-ers then determine how, as experts, to model the operations or steps for their students, how to provide effective opportunities for students to prac-tice and receive helpful feedback on the operations or steps, how to assess student progress, and how to share results with other teachers in the pro-gram or discipline. The steps needed to get through the bottleneck may be identified in a Decoding interview by inquiring of the teacher interviewee what steps she took in overcoming the difficulty when she was a learner or apprentice herself, or by asking her what an expert would do to overcome the difficulty, or both (Díaz et al. 2008).

Decoding the Disciplines interviews conducted with faculty members at Mount Royal University (described in Miller-Young and Boman, Chapter 2) bumped up against not only the interviewees' professional identities as teachers, always by definition in play in the interviews but specifically their disciplinary professional identities as, say, nurses or journalists. Interview-ers in these situations (including the present author) did not pursue discus-sion of disciplinary professional identities as such in much depth or breadth. We might have done, though, because unpacking the ways and means by which disciplinary professional identities are constructed and frame pro-fessional practices has the potential to reveal important knowledge often hidden from the identities' bearers and, therefore, from their students who are trying to find their way into the professions and disciplines in question.

NEW DIRECTIONS FOR TEACHING AND LEARNING, no. 150, Summer 2017 © 2017 Wiley Periodicals, Inc.
Published online in Wiley Online Library (wileyonlinelibrary.com) • DOI: 10.1002/tl.20238

The principal purpose of this chapter is to suggest how key concep-tualizations of identity in contemporary variants of identity theory might offer tools with which Decoding interviewers could explore professional disciplinary identities more deeply and widely, thus uncovering additional elements of interviewees' professional tacit knowledge that otherwise go unreflected and remain mysterious to students.

Identity and Learning

Connections between higher learning and identity are increasingly well es-tablished and are understood in increasingly complex ways. Psychology un-dergraduates who self-identify strongly as psychology students have been shown to learn more deeply, and their deeper learning has been shown to further strengthen their self-identity as psychology students (Platow, Mavor, and Grace 2013). Teaching to foster in students "the disposition to learn for oneself" and the ability to monitor one's own learning and studying and to adapt these activities to make them as effective as possible are key in the practice of excellent teachers and manifestly engage students' identities as students (Entwistle 2009).

Learning often or perhaps always is "initiation into a practice," among other things, and any practice is "intertwined" in a specific way or ways with the learner's self and sense of identity (Smeyers and Burbules 2006, 448–449):

> Some practices thrive on the possibility of multiple or alternative identities; others exemplify and enforce a more static identity. In both cases our relations to others and to ourselves will be changed. Practices transform the self. (449)

In other words, learning in professions is taking on "professional ways of being" (Dall'Alba 2009a, 2009b). Higher learning means entering into "the roles of the game" (Tandoc 2014).

Prediger (2001) offers what might be considered a limit argument as to the involvement of identity in learning. She argues, and cites others in mathematics, philosophy, and anthropology in support, that mathematics, the discipline that might be considered the purest of all in terms of learn-ing, actually needs to be understood as a culture, "and whenever we ex-pect students to learn mathematics they are confronted with an intercultural learning situation" (163):

> [T]his perspective runs counter to the classical approach to mathematics, which views it as objective science, in which ultimate truths are discovered and indubitable knowledge is collected in a cumulative fashion. . . . [E]ven in mathematics, results are sometimes falsified, and the main criterion for the correctness of mathematical proof is social acceptance within the community (165).

NEW DIRECTIONS FOR TEACHING AND LEARNING • DOI: 10.1002/tl

Prediger (2001) notes that intercultural learning cannot confine itself to the cognitive realm but must also address and if possible change attitudes and behavior. Students must learn "what specific characteristics are associated with the mathematical approach to the world," how to apply "mathematical strategies and concepts to everyday thinking," and how to look at the world through "mathematical glasses" (167–168). The achievement of these aims is an intercultural enterprise because students come to the table already immersed in, constructing their identities in, their everyday cultures.

All of the ways in which identity is entangled in learning make hurdles, often very high hurdles, for students, and although the learning and teaching element of this entanglement has received much attention, not as much work has been done on understanding the identity element. The relatively less thorough exploration of the identity element in learning matters for two significant reasons.

First, a new identity, or new, important aspects of identity, can be very difficult for students to take on board. Two of the originators of the Decoding the Disciplines process have reported with colleagues on their exploration of one key aspect of students' identities in the Indiana University Affective Learning Project (ALP). That research identified emotional barriers to student acquisition of disciplinary professional ways of thinking in the discipline of history and noted a growing literature on the affective dimensions of conceptual change. A key source of the emotional learning bottlenecks analyzed in the Indiana ALP was the preconceptions students brought into the tertiary classroom from their primary and secondary school experiences of learning history and from their out-of-school lives in specific class, ethnic, racial, and other social locations (Middendorf et al. 2015).

A second reason the relatively less thorough exploration of the identity element in learning matters is because important parts of that element may be invisible to experts already established in a discipline: the identity is lived rather than being necessarily reflected upon. Experts, then, face some difficulty in helping their students over the identity hurdle.

Professional Identities in Decoding Interviews

It has been notable in Decoding the Disciplines bottleneck interviews conducted at Mount Royal University how readily the interviews have encountered aspects of interviewees' disciplinary professional identities. Two examples show what is meant.

A Decoding interview with a nursing teacher and professional nurse whom we call Louisa concerned a chronic problem in a foundational introduction to pathophysiology and pharmacology: students had persistent difficulty in relating what they learned about processes in the human body at the cellular level to symptoms of illnesses they were expected to diagnose. Following Decoding the Disciplines practice, interviewers asked Louisa to think about her own ways of thinking and practicing when it came to diagnosing illness. There was discussion about whether nurses typically in practice would think about a patient's symptoms on the cellular level and relate cellular-level thinking to the symptoms. Louisa said many nurses would not think through the problem on a cellular level. Interviewers pursued the matter.

> *Interviewer: Does ... a nurse—a practicing nurse—day to day need to know those cellular processes? What does a nurse on a ward do, versus what you are asking them to do in the class?*

> When we are teaching it is sort of backwards to the way nurses work on the unit, because nurses working on the unit need to make decisions quickly, and it is all about being able to know what you need to look at in order to make a decision in order to take care of a patient properly. . . Often times students are in the dark about that because they don't have the experience to feed back on.

Discussion ensued around the complexity of the relations between cellular theory and nursing practice, Louisa concluding that what she might be asking students to view as a linear process in her classes is not in practice anything like a linear process and is further complicated when considering the social factors affecting the patient. Louisa was asked to describe how she learned diagnostic practice as a nurse.

> I learned a lot from my practice in Emerg when I first started there . . . . My first day I brought my textbooks thinking that if I had a patient I would look things up and figure it out, and I remember a nurse there said, "Put those away! You are not going to be looking that up!" and then . . . literally I was taking care of patients by noticing what I saw and learning from some constellation of symptoms and . . . signs.

> *Interviewer: Does one get better and better at that kind of thing?*

> I think so . . . because . . . they develop an intuition and they have taken care of a patient before and like, "I can't put my finger on that, but I know there is some thing wrong and I know that patient is going to go sour," and sure enough that patient goes sour even though they don't have any clear indication, they can't back it up with any evidence, they just have a feeling . . . and that is when an expert is talking.

Louisa's skills as a nurse are lived. Nurses' intuition is a celebrated element of nurses' disciplinary professional identities and a subject of theorizing in nursing scholarship (Payne 2015).

NEW DIRECTIONS FOR TEACHING AND LEARNING • DOI: 10.1002/tl

A Decoding interview with a journalism teacher and professional journalist we call Bonnie focused on her students' difficulties in developing ideas for good news stories. The ability to develop ideas for interesting, topical news stories is fundamental to success as a journalist. The ability has names in journalism practice—a nose for news, gut instinct, and it is a subject of theorizing in journalism scholarship (Kronstad 2014; Schultz 2007). Bonnie was asked why, in her view, students lacked the nose for news.

> They don't seem to hear and see the things that I think as a journalist I hear and see. When I have a conversation with someone over the years I have realized—it is really tough on my friends and my circle of acquaintances—but everything you say is potential fodder for a story idea.

What else goes into Bonnie's acute ability to develop good news stories?

> When working actively as a journalist . . . I stay abreast of what other people are doing in terms of news content, and in the way that I engage with that content in terms of story ideas is that I am constantly looking for what do they cover? What are the gaps? What is it that follows? . . . What did they miss? Who did they not talk to?' Often what they miss is a face of the story, or people who are marginalized or disenfranchised, and that is often a big missing piece for me.

How does Bonnie know to ask those kinds of questions?

> I am not sure, like how is it that I just know? I just know . . . and I think maybe being well read and being on the planet for a little while certainly contributes to helping identify this stuff. . . from a cultural studies side of things, or critical studies really, I am aware that there are haves and have-nots, I am aware there are power differentials.

Further exploration with Bonnie of the significant difference between her own instinct for good news stories, clearly a key element of her professional disciplinary identity as a journalist, and her students' profound difficulty in developing a similar instinct ran into the affective dimension of failed professional disciplinary identity formation, an emotional bottleneck.

> Those unexplored angles . . . when you pull them up to the surface they are typically tension laden. . . And this is the part that the students . . . are afraid of the tension and they are . . . "Oh, you just want a lot of negative stories," and it is no, I want tension-filled stories! . . . They seem afraid of the tension, they seem afraid of the negativity and afraid of the conflict.

NEW DIRECTIONS FOR TEACHING AND LEARNING • DOI: 10.1002/tl

A professional journalist's so-called "nose for news," her ability to spot (or construct) a story that needs to be told, is an example of an attribute central to her disciplinary professional identity but profoundly difficult for her students to acquire.

The journalist's nose for news and nurse's intuition are key elements of the specific perspectives on reality with which these professional disciplines operate. They are key elements, too, of the lived disciplinary professional identities of journalists and nurses. Students in journalism and nursing programs are being directed into those lived disciplinary professional identities in spite of the cognitive and emotional learning bottlenecks encountered along the way.

The process as it stands, however, is seriously inefficient. Time is wasted and emotional prices are paid trying to get through the bottlenecks. Some students do not get through and so do not realize their dreams of becoming journalists or nurses. So long as key elements like the nose for news and nurse's intuition are acquired more or less unconsciously, by repetition, by emulation in the workplace, by the gradual acquisition of disciplinary languages, the resulting disciplinary professional identities are likely to be largely the same as last year's, and those of the year before, and the year before that (Stibbe 2011).

The acquisition of professional disciplinary identities might usefully become a fully conscious process, a process reflected upon critically by its subjects, a process deconstructed and open to change by its subjects. Introducing insights from identity theory into the decoding interviews could help open doors to such understandings as where the nose for news or nurse's intuition comes from, of what roles they play in journalists' or nurses' professional identities, or of how they contribute or fail to contribute to the futures of the disciplines.

Identity Theory

Contemporary identity theory offers potential help for interviewers and interviewees exploring disciplinary professional identities as part of a Decoding the Disciplines process. Ordinary-life reflections on identity may be said to focus most often on relatively coherent, steady-state conceptualizations with limited or even singular aspects and originating paths. But the cultural theorist Stuart Hall has noted that this kind of everyday conceptualization of identity prevails "only because we construct a comforting story or 'narrative of the self' about ourselves" (1996, 598). (Not all such stories, of course, are necessarily comforting.) In contrast, identity theory in all of its various flavors conceptualizes identity as always evolving, many-sided, multivoiced, situational, with both self-reflected and unreflected elements, and arising from a multitrack set or system of origins.

NEW DIRECTIONS FOR TEACHING AND LEARNING • DOI: 10.1002/tl

Instead of asking what are people's roots, we ought to think about what are their routes, the different points by which they have come to be now; they are, in a sense, the sum of those differences. . . . These routes hold us in places, but what they don't do is hold us in the same place. We need to try to make sense of the connections with where we think we were then as compared to where we are now. That is what . . . the stories we tell ourselves or the autobiographies we write are meant to do, to convince ourselves that these are not a series of leaps in the dark that we took, but they did have some logic . . .a logic of connected meaning. (Hall 1999, 2)

Narrative Identity Theory. Narrative identity theory is particularly concerned with those routes Hall suggests we consider. Narrative identity theory is about how and why humans establish meaning in their own and others' lives through storytelling and, in the process, become agents in building their own and others' identities, always within specific social-cultural contexts (Brockmeier and Carbaugh 2001). Narrative identity theory in its strongest expressions posits that identity cannot be thought, indeed may not even be possible, without narrative construction.

Discovering the narrative routes by which people construct identities is not a simple matter. People follow more than one narrative route in constructing their identities, and they construct multiple identities and construct those identities repeatedly. Individuals' narratives of self include both real and fictive elements (Brockmeier and Harré 2001). The constituents and elements of narrative structures in individuals' self-stories: plots, storylines, points of view, characters, voices and genres; and the structures themselves are flexible and unstable (Brockmeier and Harré 2001; Freeman and Brockmeier 2001).

It is an essential characteristic of narrative to be a highly sensitive guide to the variable and fleeting nature of human reality because it is, in part, constitutive of it. . . . The study of narrative invites us to rethink the whole issue of the Heraclitean nature of human experience because it works as an open and malleable frame that enables us to come to terms with an ever-changing, ever reconstructed reality. (Brockmeier and Harré 2001, 53).

Precisely as an open and malleable frame, the narrative frame offers means of understanding the ever-changing, ever reconstructed reality that is anyone's disciplinary professional identity or "set" of always provisional disciplinary professional identities.

Not all of an identity is narrated consciously by its bearer. The stories of any individual's disciplinary professional identities are shaped by the individual's own struggles to make sense of her life, and, without the individual necessarily being at all or wholly conscious of the fact, by taken-for-granted models, by social-organizational constraints, by listeners' reactions, and by those who tell stories to and about the storyteller (Gregg 2006; Holstein and

Gubrium 2000; Laing 1993; Pasupathi 2006; Shoemaker and Reese 2014). In what today is for most people an extremely complex lived world, an identity is an ongoing enterprise constantly in revision and requiring constant maintenance (Holstein and Gubrium 2000).

Sociological Components of Identity.   A thoroughly developed and empirically founded theory of how identities actually operate is offered by Burke and Stets (2009) through the lens of sociological social psychology. Relying on the results of more than a decade of research, they characterize an identity as being made up of a system of "four basic components: an *input*, an *identity standard*, a *comparator*, and an *output*" (62, italics in original). A person's identities are maintained or altered by the operation of these components in a "constant loop": perceptions (inputs) from the environment of, say, how feminine a person's behaviors are, are compared (comparator) with the person's understanding of what feminine behaviors should be (identity standard) and new behaviors are executed (outputs) to maintain the feminine identity or to improve or alter it. The system is in default conservative, working to maintain or verify the identity in relatively close alignment with the identity standard.

The operation of this system for maintaining or altering an identity can be studied empirically, determining the bases, influences, and evolutions of the meanings by which the identity-bearer orders her world, the meanings conveyed to or imposed upon her by the social structures she lives and by her interactions with others, the resources she draws upon to maintain or strengthen her identity, the agency she exerts in deciding to strengthen or weaken an identity by, say, increasing or reducing her commitment to a particular role, and the processes by which she maintains her multiple identities (teacher, biologist, life partner, feminist, manager) in a sustainable totality. The Burke-Stets system opens the door, too, to studying the affective as well as the cognitive elements and processes of identity verification and identity change.

Dialogical Self Theory.   Important help in grasping the complexities of the processes by which people maintain or alter, or suffer the maintenance or alteration, of their multiple identities, especially as these processes are further complicated by the globalization of relevant factors, is offered by dialogical self theory (Hermans and Hermans-Konopka 2010). Dialogical self theory is interested in how people position their selves in global as well as local contexts. It is dialogical theory because it conceives the person

> in terms of a dynamic multiplicity of I-positions or voices in the landscape of the mind, intertwined as this mind is with the minds of other people... Dialogues may take place among internal positions in the self (e.g., "As an answer to the conflict between my position as a father and my position as

a hardworking scientist I found a workable solution"), between internal and external positions of the self (e.g., "as the son of my father I'm used to talking with him about my successes and disappointments") and between external positions of the self (e.g., "Two colleagues . . . solved their serious conflict and I learned a lot from that"). (32)

Dialogical self theory reads emotions and the self as mutually constitutive. It suggests there is a dialogical relationship worth studying in depth between the emotional "I" and the reasonable "I." It regards the emotional processes constitutive of the self as complex, staged processes open to analysis.

Decoding Identity

In the tapestry of identity theories available to contemporary researchers, the fundamental stake is the tension between the social construction of identity and the self-construction of identity. In Decoding the Disciplines interviews, and the follow-on elements of the Decoding process, the ultimate stake is the ability of students to acquire, by way of conceptual change among other things, the ways of thinking, practicing, and being specific to the discipline in question. The available identity theories (and the descriptions provided here are only a limited, partial account of just some aspects of some theories) in their current states of development offer conceptual tools for detailed analysis of identity, including analysis of how students acquire disciplinary professional identity.

From narrative identity theory, Decoding interviewers could have invoked lines of discussion aimed at elaborating the interviewees' stories of how, when, and why their perspectives on reality changed as their professional identities developed; of what meanings they had ascribed to their lives and how and why these had changed in light of the development of their professional identities; of when and how they believed they had been agents in constructing their own or others' professional identities; and of when and how they had felt themselves to have had little choice in constructing their professional identities.

Narrative identity theory could inspire discussions of how interviewees' professional development had followed particular plot lines, involved certain characters in certain roles, lent itself to being understood via certain tropes, encountered specific challenges en route, and been sidetracked or followed different routes at different times (such as professional versus teacher identities).

Narrative identity theory could open the door to exploring how the discourse of journalism practice or of nursing practice shapes professional identity and of how that discourse might be changed to offer different models of professional practice and professional identity. Decoding interviewers might begin exploring narrative identity by asking, "If you were asked to tell the story of how you became a true professional as a journalist, where would you begin?" Developing the interviewee's story, interviewers might ask, "What metaphors would you use to describe the most difficult parts of becoming a professional as a nurse?"

Identity theory founded in sociological social psychology could direct interviewers to exploring Burke's and Stets' four basic components of identity. Interviewers and interviewees thus could try to identify the inputs to professional journalism or nursing identity, the identity standards against which these disciplinary identities are measured, the machinery for maintaining the identities in question, and the outputs of those disciplinary professional identities. Each of these elements could be addressed critically: what changes might be warranted, what aspects might be found missing, what agency is permitted to the identity's bearer, what are the affective dimensions of the identities seen through a Burke-Stets lens? A Decoding interviewer working with Burke's and Stets' schema could ask, "What are the key resources you call upon to maintain your professional identity as a journalist in the face of challenges to that identity?" Exploration of the dimensions of professional identity more felt than reflected might start with, "What are the most important elements of a nurse's professional identity that are discussed by nurses only informally, if at all?"

Dialogical self theory could inspire exploration of the interior and exterior conversations constitutive of journalists' and nurses' professional identities. When and where had these conversations occurred in interviewees' experiences? Which of these conversations were useful and which were not? What conflicts or synergies had been noticed between professional identity and other identities and how had these been confronted or exploited? Interesting questions might be asked in light of a dialogical theory of professional identity. "Do you have more than one kind of journalist inhabiting your journalist's professional being?" "What conversations does your private, personal self have with your professional nurse's self around how you want others to see you?"

Through all of these discussions, interviewers and interviewees would be looking constantly for the constitutive elements of the disciplinary professional identities at issue, and for the interplay between the emotional "I" and the reasonable "I" on each stage of the journeys to those identities, all in order to enable discussion and instruction with students. For Decoders, the proposals made here can constitute a rich program of learning, research, and development and ultimately a boon for students.

References

Brockmeier, Jens, and Donal Carbaugh. 2001. "Introduction." In *Narrative and Identity: Studies in Autobiography, Self and Culture*, edited by Jens Brockmeier and Donal Carbaugh, 1–24. Amsterdam: John Benjamins.

Brockmeier, Jens, and Rom Harré. 2001. "Narrative: Problems and Promises of an Alternative Paradigm." In *Narrative and Identity: Studies in Autobiography, Self and*

Culture, edited by Jens Brockmeier and Donald Carbaugh, 39–58. Amsterdam: John Benjamins.

Burke, Peter J., and Jan E. Stets. 2009. *Identity Theory*. Oxford, UK: Oxford University Press.

Dall'Alba, Gloria. 2009a. "Learning Professional Ways of Being: Ambiguities of Becoming." *Educational Philosophy and Theory* 41 (1): 34–45.

Dall'Alba, Gloria. 2009b. *Learning to Be Professionals*. New York: Springer.

Díaz, Arlene, Joan Middendorf, David Pace, and Leah Shopkow. 2008. "The History Learning Project: A Department 'Decodes' Its Students." *Journal of American History* 94 (4): 1211–1224.

Entwistle, Noel. 2009. *Teaching for Understanding at University: Deep Approaches and Distinctive Ways of Thinking*. Houndmills, Basingstoke: Palgrave Macmillan.

Freeman, Mark, and Jens Brockmeier. 2001. "Narrative Integrity: Autobiographical Identity and the Meaning of the "Good Life." In *Narrative and Identity: Studies in Autobiography, Self and Culture*, edited by Jens Brockmeier and Donald Carbaugh, 75–99. Amsterdam: John Benjamins.

Gregg, Gary S. 2006. "The Raw and the Bland: A Structural Model of Narrative Identity." In *Identity and Story: Creating Self in Narrative*, edited by Dan P. McAdams, Ruthellen Josselson, and Amia Lieblich, 63–87. Washington, DC: American Psychological Association.

Hall, Stuart. 1996. "The Question of Cultural Identity." In *Modernity: An Introduction to Modern Societies*, edited by Stuart Hall, David Held, Don Hubert, and Kenneth Thompson, 595–634. Oxford, UK: Blackwell.

Hall, Stuart. 1999. "A Conversation with Stuart Hall." *Journal of the International Institute* 7 (1), 1–7. Ann Arbor: University of Michigan.

Hermans, Hubert, and Agnieszka Hermans-Konopka. 2010. *Dialogical Self Theory: Positioning and Counter-Positioning in a Globalizing Society*. Cambridge, UK: Cambridge University Press.

Holstein, James A., and Jaber F. Gubrium. 2000. *The Self We Live By: Narrative Identity in a Postmodern World*. Oxford, UK: Oxford University Press.

Kronstad, Morten. 2014. "Using the Gut Feeling—Making Sense of Practical Knowledge in Journalism Education." *Journal of Media Practice* 15 (3): 176–189.

Laing, Milli. 1993. "Gossip: Does It Play a Role in the Socialization of Nurses?" *Journal of Nursing Scholarship* 25 (1): 37–44.

Middendorf, Joan, Jolanta Mickute, Tara Saunders, José Najar, Andrew E. Clark-Huckstep, and David Pace, with Keith Eberly and Nicole McGrath. 2015. "What's Feeling Got to Do with It? Decoding Emotional Bottlenecks in the History Classroom." *Arts and Humanities in Higher Education* 14 (2): 166–180.

Pace, David, and Joan Middendorf, eds. 2004. *New Directions for Teaching and Learning: No. 98. Decoding the Disciplines: Helping Students Learn Disciplinary Ways of Thinking*. San Francisco: Jossey-Bass.

Pasupathi, Monisha. 2006. "Silk from Sows' Ears: Collaborative Construction of Everyday Selves in Everyday Stories." In *Identity and Story: Creating Self in Narrative*, edited by Dan P. McAdams, Ruthellen Josselson, and Amia Lieblich, 129–150. Washington, DC: American Psychological Association.

Payne, Leslie Karns. 2015. "Towards a Theory of Intuitive Decision-Making in Nursing." *Nursing Science Quarterly* 28 (3): 223–228.

Platow, Michael J., Kenneth I. Mavor, and Diana M. Grace. 2013. "On the Role of Discipline-Related Self-Concept in Deep and Surface Approaches to Learning among University Students." *Instructional Science* 41 (2): 271–285.

Prediger, Susanna. 2001. "Mathematics Is Also Intercultural Learning." *Intercultural Education* 12 (2): 163–171.

Schultz, Ida. 2007. "The Journalistic Gut Feeling: Journalistic Doxa, News Habitus and Orthodox News Values." *Journalism Practice* 1 (2): 190-207.

Shoemaker, Pamela J., and Stephen D. Reese. 2014. *Mediating the Message in the 21st Century: A Media Sociology Perspective*, 3rd ed. London: Routledge.

Smeyers, Paul, and Nicholas C. Burbules. 2006. "Education as Initiation into Practices." *Educational Theory* 56 (4): 439–449.

Stibbe, Arran. 2011. "Identity Reflection: Students and Societies in Transition." *Learning and Teaching in Higher Education* 5: 86–95.

Tandoc, Edson C. Jr. 2014. "The *Roles* of the Game: The Influence of News Consumption Patterns on the Role Conceptions of Journalism Students." *Journalism and Mass Communication Educator* 69 (3): 256–270.

RON MACDONALD, *now retired, was a college and university teacher of political science, political philosophy, and journalism for 35 years. He was a working journalist for 30 years.*

NEW DIRECTIONS FOR TEACHING AND LEARNING • DOI: 10.1002/tl

This chapter describes a multidisciplinary faculty self-study about reciprocity in service-learning. The study began with each coauthor participating in a Decoding interview. We describe how Decoding combined with collaborative self-study had a positive impact on our teaching practice.

6

Building Bridges from the Decoding Interview to Teaching Practice

Jennifer Pettit, Melanie Rathburn, Victoria Calvert, Roberta Lexier, Margot Underwood, Judy Gleeson, Yasmin Dean

In February 2014, fourteen students and two professors traveled to the remote jungles of Honduras to participate in a global service-learning project. Upon consultation with community leaders, it was determined that footbridges would be built along a flooded path to ensure that the children in the community could safely walk to school. Believing that this initial consultation meant working with the community rather than dictating what should be done for them, the group got to work, collecting materials from the surrounding jungle and beginning to construct bridges. Very quickly, however, it became apparent that the students and professors were ill equipped to build effective bridges; the construction was incredibly difficult and the roads continuously flooded despite their best efforts. Throughout the morning, members of the community began congregating around the construction sites, watching the lack of progress and laughing at the group's efforts. Realizing that the locals had tremendous knowledge and experience, the group began to consult with them to determine the best way to construct bridges that would actually meet the needs of the community. Moreover, the locals began to assist with the construction. By the end of the day, the group, in collaboration with local community members, had built a number of bridges that provided the children with a dry path to reach their school. Working *with* the community was substantially more effective than working *for* them. This experience made the faculty members question their grasp of the concept of reciprocity, something integral to community service-learning projects and a concept they originally felt they understood.

The experience of this group of students and their professors, two coauthors of this chapter, is all too common and not an isolated incident.

NEW DIRECTIONS FOR TEACHING AND LEARNING, no. 150, Summer 2017 © 2017 Wiley Periodicals, Inc.
Published online in Wiley Online Library (wileyonlinelibrary.com) • DOI: 10.1002/tl.20239

This is not surprising given that it has been argued that "service learning pedagogy requires and fosters learning—often transformational, paradigm-shifting learning—on the part of everyone involved, including faculty" (Clayton, Bringle, and Hatcher 2013, 245). Indeed, given that service-learning necessitates faculty giving up control and working reciprocally with partners, sometimes much more than bridges need to be shifted and changed. Recognizing this, and because of our commitment to developing our teaching practice, we, the authors of this article, set out to investigate our own thinking with regard to reciprocity through a collaborative self-study, which included the use of a Decoding interview (Pace and Middendorf 2004).

Our initial research examined how the Decoding interview followed by our self-study process generated learning about reciprocity specifically (Miller-Young et al. 2015). In this chapter we report how Decoding had an impact on four areas of our teaching practice: (1) our identity and role as teachers, especially in an experiential learning setting; (2) the discovery of similarities and differences we shared with colleagues from diverse disciplines; (3) new strategies for forging meaningful and truly reciprocal relationships with partners in global service-learning field schools; and (4) our design, delivery, and assessment in field schools.

Background and Methods

Our self-study stemmed from the creation of a multidisciplinary collaborative faculty learning community on service-learning in field schools. In particular, motivated by experiences such as the one in Honduras described previously, we had a common purpose (Schoenfeld 1999)—we were curious to explore the similarities and differences among our field schools and we wanted to analyze the different ways that we approached reciprocity in these service-learning courses (see also Miller-Young et al. 2015). We also attempted to at least partially address Kreber's (2013) argument that the scholarship of teaching and learning has not lived up to its potential as it "has not adequately taken up the bigger questions of social justice and equality *in* and *through* higher education" (Kreber 2013, 3).

Our group members varied in our level of experience with service-learning and faculty-led field schools, and we came from a range of disciplinary backgrounds. Our field schools were equally diverse (see author biographies at the end of this chapter for further information). Kitchen and Ciuffetelli Parker (2009) maintain that the self-study methodology is particularly effective within this collaborative type of community of practice. Indeed, Louie and colleagues argue that

> when compared to participation in traditional teaching workshops, self-study research has numerous benefits. It specifically addresses the faculty member's teaching context, including the subject matter, student population, and other

unique aspects of a class. Rather than playing the role of passive participants, faculty members engaged in self-study research actively control the purpose, agenda, and timing of their work as well as its outcomes. Self-study research also enables faculty members to create a tangible product from their work in the form of teaching knowledge that is transferable to colleagues. (Louie et al. 2003, 51)

Global Service-Learning (GSL) and Reciprocity.   Service-learning has been described by many as "a high impact teaching practice," one in which students "learn more, gain better understanding and application of the course material, improve writing and critical thinking skills, and can better apply course principles to new situations." (Wilsey et al. 2014, 79, 81). Clearly service-learning can have a beneficial impact on students, but it is not without its faults. As Stoecker and Tryon (2009) explain, "there has been growing dissatisfaction among people both inside and outside the service learning movement since the 1990s, particularly when it comes to the issue of whether service learning truly serves communities" (5). Faculty who lead GSL activities are typically motivated by a sincere belief in the potential for positive reciprocal relationships with community partners (Hartman and Kiely 2014; Sharpe and Dear 2013). Yet, faculty involved in GSL need to critically reflect on the extent to which they are actually involved in reciprocal relationships. Although some models to guide practice have been developed (such as Leffers and Mitchell 2011), more remains to be done. Hence our desire to study and deepen our own thinking about the concept of reciprocity and how it affected our teaching practice.

Our Self-Study Process.   The Decoding the Disciplines model was initially created to help faculty articulate, and subsequently to help students learn, discipline-specific ways of thinking through the study of a "bottleneck" or difficult concepts. Typically Decoding uses a cross-disciplinary format to study ways of operating in a discipline, such as history, political science, or music (see, for instance, Bernstein 2012; Burkholder 2011; Díaz et al. 2007). However, we discovered that Decoding can also assist faculty in articulating and reflecting upon their thinking about a difficult concept which they themselves struggle with (Miller-Young et al. 2015), which in turn can have an impact upon teaching practice. Our data come from three sources and two phases of self-study. First, we each participated in a Decoding interview in which we were repeatedly asked to delve more deeply and to better explain our ideas and claims about reciprocity in our courses. Second, self-study group members wrote two individual written reflections, one of which was written after reading the transcription of each individual's Decoding interview and another after a group discussion. In the second phase of our study, over a year after we conducted our Decoding interviews, we engaged in recorded group discussions where we focused on the changes we had made to practice as a result of our study.

The Impact of Our Decoding Self-Study

At the conclusion of this second phase of our self-study, we determined that the Decoding process and self-study had a significant influence upon four main areas of our teaching practice.

Our Identity and Role as Teachers, Particularly in an Experiential Learning Setting.   The first area upon which the Decoding process had an influence was our identity and role as teachers. Interviews, reflections, and group discussions often revealed that in order to be successful in the setting of field schools, we needed to adopt an approach different to that typically taken in a traditional classroom setting. This counternormative nature of service-learning that positions faculty, students, and community partners simultaneously as both learners and teachers (Sigmon 1979) and that invites all of these partners into unfamiliar and challenging reciprocal relationships as cocreators, can be disconcerting because of academic norms that "reinforce the distinct identities of faculty as educators and generators of knowledge, students as learners, and community members as recipients of academic expertise" (Clayton et al. 2013, 246). Yet Boyer (1990 as cited in Leibowitz and Bozalek 2015, 11) has argued that "good teaching means that faculty, as scholars, are also learners."

Pettit explained in the last group discussion that "it is humbling how little you know sometimes, and how much people share with you and are willing to share with you." Likewise, through Decoding Pettit learned that she was actually not as in control of the field school as she initially supposed to be the case, as did Calvert: "I am used to being in a structured environment where I can control the A, B, C . . . and I control the assessment . . . and then we go through something like this and reflect upon it deeply and you realize, 'You are 10 percent of this. Maybe 15.' . . . as a professor in a structured course, we are the drivers. In a course like this I feel more like a conduit." Gleeson fittingly explained that "if we are trying to model this idea that reciprocity is important and that we are working in partnerships, then being top down with the students is not going to work."

Interestingly, self-study participants also realized that the Decoding process revealed more than information about their teaching practice. Lexier, for example, in the final discussion described how "a lot of what came out of my Decoding interview was about my own activism and why I do what I do, and it became much more of an internal focus . . . The Decoding process for me was really good both in terms of understanding what the heck we are really doing when we go to Honduras, but also understanding my own internal dynamics and why this is what I am doing." Calvert also explained that Decoding "helped me crystalize. 'Ah, this is what I am doing here. This is my value. This is why I am motivated to come and work.'" In

NEW DIRECTIONS FOR TEACHING AND LEARNING • DOI: 10.1002/tl

other words, our interviews and reflections gave us a venue within which we could reflect upon topics beyond our teaching practice. This came as a surprise to many, as did the impact, both positive and negative, of coming from a variety of disciplines and types of field schools.

Discovery of Similarities and Differences We Shared with Colleagues from Diverse Disciplines. Using the Decoding interview to launch a self-study composed of faculty from a variety of disciplines was not without difficulties. At the start of the study, disciplinary differences that ranged from simple misunderstandings about terminology to significant differences in methodologies and theoretical approaches seemed like they might be barriers to learning. At the end of the entire Decoding process Pettit described her attendance at the first Decoding group meeting in the following way: "I was terrified at that first meeting... I didn't think we had any commonality at all." Similarly, midway through the process Calvert explained that "this experience has been like a trip to a foreign culture. One of the challenges is the process itself—it is not linear, it is spiral with feedback loops. In my previous experience, I controlled the process and created a linear structure with a finite sequential process and deadlines... The peek into the values and assumptions of faculty in other disciplines has been a bit surprising." At the start of the study, Rathburn was also concerned about her ability to effectively contribute to the group due to disciplinary differences. In her reflection on the process she noted: "I felt there was a huge disciplinary divide—they were talking about social justice and I remember sitting in the car thinking 'What is social justice and how do I even fit into this?'...The language used by those in the 'caring fields' is very different than what I am used to and that was a bit unsettling."

As the Decoding process unfolded, however, shared experiences, values, and characteristics emerged (Miller-Young et al. 2015). In the final discussion Underwood explained that "we shifted to a commonality that we didn't start with." Indeed, one of the major strengths of this group, according to every participant, was the perspectives and values from different disciplines that helped to inform our understanding of reciprocity. For example, despite initial misgivings, Lexier later claimed that "while it has been difficult sometimes to understand other approaches and where people are coming from... it has been incredibly positive to do that." Similarly, Gleeson stated: "I think the fact that there are people from different perspectives and different academic disciplines has been great because we learn a lot from each other; even though we have the same kind of issues, we have different lenses." Dean reiterated this point in her reflection on the group dynamics: "This cross pollination of ideas is incredibly deep and is fully shaping my work and professional and personal identities... I am getting increasingly aware of my own thinking and approaches." Likewise, in the final discussion Lexier reiterated that "we had shared values. That is what brought us together. The values we wanted to implement in our field schools."

One of the most important values that faculty sought to realize in their field schools was forging respectful reciprocal relationships with partners in service-learning courses. Again, the Decoding process revealed how best we could do this, the result of which was a deeper understanding of reciprocity and the specific changes that needed to be made to the relationships with our partners.

New Strategies for Forming Meaningful and Truly Reciprocal Relationships with Partners in Global Service-Learning Field Schools.   For Dean, Pettit, Gleeson, and Underwood, for whom reciprocal approaches were part of their disciplinary training, reciprocity was not a new concept, but the Decoding interview and ensuing activities caused them to question their assumptions about whether or not they were fully enacting the concept in their partnerships. Thus, even for study participants for whom reciprocity was a concept that was integral to their disciplinary training, the Decoding method provided new insights about reciprocity and teaching practice. Perhaps most important, our collaborative reflections helped us all to more clearly see the importance of working *with* and not *for* our community partners (Clayton et al. 2013); that as Calvert explained in the last group discussion, "we need to focus on the partner in partnership." We realized that we needed to more fully respect and appreciate what our partners give our students, rather than simply focusing on what we contribute to our partners through service-learning projects. As a result of this more comprehensive and deeper knowledge about reciprocity, we determined a number of specific changes in our relationships and dealings with our community partners that needed to be made.

To begin, we learned to be less leery about overworking our partners. Rathburn, for instance, realized that she "must be more strategic and intentional with my partners and I need to include them in all aspects of the service-learning project. Part of my thinking was to not add any additional workload to partners, but I realize I was missing out on a huge opportunity to collaborate meaningfully." Similarly, Underwood learned that "only if you are really engaged with a partner, and you are both involved in planning the course that you are moved to a high level of showing reciprocity."

We also recognized that we needed to spend more time prior to the field schools brainstorming with our partners, ideally in a face-to-face setting. In addition, rather than telling our partners what we thought would work, we allowed them to take control, which resulted in more meaningful experiences for both them and students. For example, in the past Pettit asked her community partners to plan specific activities. After the Decoding process she instead asked her partners to organize what they thought best and what they wanted to do, and the result was a much more elaborate and meaningful activity: "They set up a traditional painted lodge tipi for us in the mountains and brought in elders and played traditional games. Those partners have since come to the university and given workshops and lectures."

NEW DIRECTIONS FOR TEACHING AND LEARNING • DOI: 10.1002/tl

We also realized that successful, sustainable, and reciprocal field schools require a longer term approach. As Calvert explained during the last group discussion, "that level of partnership will only work if you have a long-term relationship." To foster this type of connection, Lexier and Rathburn, for instance, now travel to Honduras even in the years in which their field school is not offered.

We also learned about the importance of sharing with our partners the impact that the field school has on field school students and beyond. At the end of the Decoding process Rathburn described how "one of the complaints that comes out of many field schools, and from people we have talked to, and from our partners in Honduras, is that volunteer groups come in, they volunteer, and they leave. Nothing ever comes back. They don't even know the outcomes." We discovered that one particularly effective way to show partners the impact of the field school was to invite them to Calgary, Alberta to our university. When Gleeson and Underwood invited their Dominican Republic partners to Calgary, for instance, their partners were taken aback when they saw posters about the field school and that a university publication had been written about the field school; Gleeson explained that "when they saw that they were thrilled ... they were surprised." Likewise, since we started this study, Pettit and her coinstructor have made a concerted effort to bring their community partners to the university, resulting in a number of co-organized events such as a speaker series and the implementation of an elder-in-residence. As Rathburn pointed out "you can bring your partners back to campus so that you are affecting not just your students, but changing an entire institution." Such visits though, also made faculty appreciate the onerous nature of their partners having to host faculty and students. Underwood described this recent experience in the following way: "We are now the hosts and feeling what they feel ... there is time and effort to make all this work. Well imagine what it feels like if you hosting eighteen people all at the same time!" In addition to making faculty reflect more fully on their relationships with partners, our study has also had an influence on curriculum design, delivery, and assessment.

Changes to Our Design, Delivery, and Assessment in Field Schools. As a result of realizing our shortcomings despite our experience and disciplinary expertise, we also realized that we could do a better job of preparing our students for service-learning. For instance, by interrogating her understanding of reciprocity, Underwood gained a better respect for the challenges that her students face when dealing with this potentially difficult topic: "It really helped clarify for me that for students, of course they are going to find this a bottleneck concept! They haven't had the experience we have had, they haven't been out there ... it reminded me not to brush it over as much as I was, and think 'Why aren't you getting this?'" Through Decoding we were reminded that field schools are about more than developing skills and content—they are about developing values and helping to create global citizens. Such integration of ways of thinking and being takes time.

We also discovered that significant changes needed to be made to our curriculum design, delivery, and assessment. One of the most important takeaways from our self-study was the value of not scripting too many things ahead of time, that serendipity has a valuable role to play in field schools. We also learned that dissonance and discomfort is not necessarily a bad thing for faculty and students. Another discovery was the importance of providing space and time for nongraded reflection and allowing students to help shape their assignments and service-learning activities. Most important, we realized that student and faculty learning is not always immediate or quantifiable. As Rathburn explained during the last group discussion, "It is nice seeing the development of students over time and the things they might not have realized at the time...one thing they are reporting during interviews that come months after field school is that it has changed how they participate in their community." We also came to an agreement that assigning grades presents a special challenge in field schools, though we did not have concrete solutions to this issue. As Pettit explained, "Sometimes it feels like we are putting a round peg in a square hole, especially when marking service learning."

Throughout our self-study we also began to think more about the needs of our students. Though field schools are relatively short in duration, our self-study helped us understand that students often need help acclimatizing back to Canada and to the university setting. Rathburn, for example, shared in our final group discussion that during recent postcourse interviews students revealed that "they couldn't talk to people here and people didn't understand what they went through." Students reported that the field school had a much larger long-term impact than they anticipated. Many expressed a desire to act as mentors for future field school participants so they could share their experiences and/or to continue their learning in advanced field schools. Our students also sought ways to sustain the relationships they had built with community partners. However, many also struggled with the effects of taking part in field school. As Pettit explained, "we have had students break down in tears when they return. They didn't realize what it felt like to be a minority. They also recognized they were not as culturally sensitive as they originally thought." As a result of reflecting more about the needs of students, many of us have included more post field school activities and meetings with students.

In addition, the self-study made us reflect more on how teaching in a field school setting could result in an impact on teaching practice beyond field school. During the final group discussion Rathburn, for example, described how new insights as a result of Decoding "changed how I approach even my classes that don't have anything to do with service-learning...It has changed how I am teaching students and how I am talking about issues, to think about multiple perspectives...I am starting to think about how this bleeds into all my other courses." Similarly, Gleeson explained that "because we have been on field schools, we see students differently."

Conclusion and Looking Forward

Fitch, Steinke, and Hudson (2013) argue that "well-designed service learning experiences serve as bridges between the curriculum and the world outside the classroom" (57). Hence, it is not only actual bridges like those described in the vignette at the beginning of this study that are of significance, but also the "bridges" or connections that need to be made between faculty, students, and host communities. Decoding combined with self-study allowed us to explore and analyze those links. As Calvert aptly pointed out during our last group discussion, "what is key is reciprocity not only between us and our partners and partners and students, but also us and our students, us and other teachers." It can be argued that the Decoding interview and self-study process we used in this study served as an impetus and enriched faculty understanding of the vexing and oft-misunderstood concept of reciprocity, which in turn had a significant impact on four important aspects of our teaching practice. This enhanced knowledge encouraged us to alter our global service-learning courses in pragmatic ways with the goal of encouraging meaningful and beneficial experiences for faculty, community partners, and students, resulting in everyone becoming colearners and coeducators. As Lexier said during the final group discussion, "this is a journey we have all grown from." Indeed, during this process of becoming critically aware about reciprocity we moved beyond notions of faculty as "expert" and generators of knowledge and instead became learners ourselves.

In addition, to validate our findings through outside perspectives, some of us are expanding upon this work. For instance, Rathburn and Lexier are currently engaged in a research study that involves interviewing students about their understanding of service-learning (Rathburn, Lexier, and Vespa, 2016), Underwood and Gleeson are exploring host partner perspectives regarding collaboration and partnership (Underwood et al. 2016), and Dean is engaged in a collaborative self-study with her students and field school's host partner, exploring all partners' experiences of reciprocity during the India field school (Dean et al. 2016). Hence, we recognize that this is a continuous process and that much remains to be learned with every new adventure we embark upon with our students and community partners at home and abroad.

Acknowledgment

All authors contributed equally to this research project but the lead author was primarily responsible for writing this manuscript.

References

Bernstein, Jeffrey. 2012. "Plowing through Bottlenecks in Political Science." In *The Scholarship of Teaching and Learning in and across the Disciplines*, edited by Kathleen McKinney, 74–92. Bloomington: Indiana University Press.

Burkholder, J. Peter. 2011. "Decoding the Discipline of Music History for Our Students." *Journal of Music History Pedagogy* 1 (2): 93–111.

Clayton, Patti H., Robert G. Bringle, and Julie A. Hatcher, eds. 2013. *Research on Service Learning: Conceptual Frameworks and Assessment*. Vol. 2A, Students and Faculty (IUPUI Series on Service Learning Research). Sterling, VA: Stylus.

Dean, Yasmin, Terence Field, Rashmi Cole, Punita Sharan, Jyoti Sharan, Marleen Dorrestijn, Sheri May, Celina Sinclair, Mikeltie Pitre, and Narayan Gopalkrishan. "Beyond the Tourist's Gaze: Towards Culturally Dynamic University-Community Partnership in International Service Learning Field Schools." Workshop presented at the Joint World Conference on Social Work, Education and Social Development, Seoul, Korea, June 2016.

Díaz, Arlene, Joan Middendorf, David Pace, and Leah Shopkow. 2008. "The History Learning Project: A Department 'Decodes' Its Students." *Journal of American History* 94 (4): 1211–1224.

Fitch, Peggy, Pamela Steinke, and Tara D. Hudson. 2013. "Research and Theoretical Perspectives on Cognitive Outcomes of Service Learning." In *Research on Service Learning: Conceptual Frameworks and Assessment*, edited by P. H. Clayton, R. C. Bringle, and J. A. Hatcher, 57–84. Sterling, VA: Stylus.

Hartman, Eric, and Richard Kiely. 2014. "Pushing Boundaries: Introduction to the Global Service-Learning Special Section." *Michigan Journal of Community Service Learning* 21 (1): 55–63.

Kitchen, Julian, and Darlene Ciuffetelli Parker. 2009. "Self-Study Communities of Practice: Developing Community, Critically Inquiring as Community." In *Self-Study Research Methodologies for Teacher Educators*, edited by C. A. Lassonde, S. Galman, and C. Kosnik, 107–128. Rotterdam: Sense Publishers.

Kreber, Caroline. 2013. *Authenticity in and Through Teaching in Higher Education: The Transformative Potential of the Scholarship of Teaching*. New York: Routledge.

Leffers, Jeanne, and Emma Mitchell. 2011. "Conceptual Model for Partnership and Sustainability in Global Health." *Public Health Nurse* 28 (1): 91–102. https://doi.org/10.1111/j.1525-1446.2010.00892.x.

Leibowitz, Brenda, and Vivienne Bozalek. 2015. "The Scholarship of Teaching and Learning from as Social Justice Perspective." *Teaching in Higher Education* 21 (2): 109–122. https://doi.org/10.1080/13562517.2015.1115971.

Louie, Belinda Y., Denise J. Drevdahl, Jill M. Purdy, and Richard W. Stackman. 2003. "Advancing the Scholarship of Teaching through Collaborative Self-Study." *Journal of Higher Education* 74 (2): 150–171.

Miller-Young, Janice, Yasmin Dean, Melanie Rathburn, Jennifer Pettit, Margot Underwood, Judy Gleeson, Roberta Lexier, Victoria Calvert, and Patti Clayton. 2015. "Decoding Ourselves: An Inquiry into Faculty Learning About Reciprocity in Service-Learning." *Michigan Journal of Community Service Learning* 22 (1): 32–47.

Pace, David, and Joan Middendorf. eds. 2004. *New Directions in Teaching and Learning: No. 98. Decoding the Disciplines: Helping Students Learn Disciplinary Ways of Thinking*. San Francisco: Jossey-Bass.

Rathburn, Melanie, Roberta Lexier, and Andrew Vespa. 2016. "Preparing Students to Learn Across the Disciplines: Pedagogical Interventions in Community-Service Learning." Paper presented at *Symposium of Scholarship of Teaching and Learning: Learning In and Across the Disciplines, Banff, Canada*, November 2016. http://hdl.handle.net/11205/305.

Schoenfeld, Alan H. 1999. "The Core, the Canon and the Development of Research Skills." In *Issues in Education Research*, edited by C. Lagemann and L. Shulman, 166–202. San Francisco: Jossey-Bass.

Sharpe, Erin K., and Samantha Dear. 2013. "Points of Discomfort: Reflection on Power and Partnerships in International Service-Learning." *Michigan Journal of Community Service Learning* 19 (2): 49–57.

Sigmon, Robert L. 1979. "Service Learning: Three Principles." *Synergist*, National Centre for Service-Learning, ACTION 8 (1): 9–11.

Stoecker, Randy, and Elizabeth Tryon. 2009. "Unheard Voices: Community Organizations and Service Learning." In *The Unheard Voices: Community Organization and Service Learning*, edited by Randy Stoecker and Elizabeth Tryon, 1–18. Philadelphia: Temple University Press.

Underwood, Margot, Judy Gleeson, Candace Konnert, Katherine Wong, and Bautista Valerio. 2016. "Global Host Partner Perspectives: Utilizing a Conceptual Model to Strengthen Collaboration with Host Partners for International Nursing Student Placements." *Public Health Nursing* 33 (4): 351–359.

Wilsey, Stephanie A., Jessica Friedrichs, Chrys Gabrich, and Ting-Ting Chung. 2014. "A Privileged Pedagogy for Privileged Students? A Preliminary Mixed-Methods Analysis Comparing First-Generation and Non-First-Generation College Students on Post-Evaluations of Service-Learning Courses." *PRISM: A Journal of Regional Engagement* 3 (4): 79–97.

JENNIFER PETTIT is chair of the Department of Humanities at Mount Royal University and a professor of history and indigenous studies. Her field school involved travel to a variety of indigenous nations in Alberta.

MELANIE RATHBURN is an associate professor at Mount Royal University who is cross-appointed into the Department of General Education and the Department of Biology. Her field school took place in Honduras.

VICTORIA CALVERT is a professor of business at Mount Royal University where she has practiced community service-learning in her courses for 20 years. Her field school took place in the Cook Islands.

ROBERTA LEXIER is an assistant professor in the Department of General Education at Mount Royal University. Roberta's field school was located in Honduras.

MARGOT UNDERWOOD is an assistant professor in the School of Nursing and Midwifery at Mount Royal University. Her field school was located in the Dominican Republic.

JUDY GLEESON is an associate professor in the School of Nursing and Midwifery at Mount Royal University. Her field school took place in the Dominican Republic.

YASMIN DEAN is an associate professor of social work in the Faculty of Health, Community and Education at Mount Royal University. Her field school was located in India.

NEW DIRECTIONS FOR TEACHING AND LEARNING • DOI: 10.1002/tl

7

This chapter demonstrates how Decoding work can be used productively within a curriculum change process to help make design decisions based on a more nuanced understanding of student learning and the relationship of a professional program to the field.

Impact of Decoding Work within a Professional Program

Michelle Yeo, Mark Lafave, Khatija Westbrook, Jenelle McAllister, Dennis Valdez, Breda Eubank

The athletic therapy (AT) group at Mount Royal University is currently engaged in a large-scale pedagogical and curricular change, moving to a competency-based approach using a clinical presentation model. This approach "uses a scenario or a clinical case as a foundation to both teach and measure a student's knowledge, skill, or ability" (Lafave et al. 2016). There have been various components to this process, including the content validation of the clinical presentations (Lafave et al., 2016) and a qualitative self-study on the curricular change process among its faculty members, which led to the development of a community of practice within the team. The community of practice that developed "was key to the curricular change process, despite it being often focused on other elements beyond curriculum, specifically, on the practice and identity of the faculty members as athletic therapists" (Yeo et al. 2016).

Michelle Yeo, a faculty developer working with the AT team, introduced the Decoding the Disciplines interview as another vehicle to delve more deeply into the team's approaches to the curriculum. All members of the team were quite intrigued by the concept and agreed it would serve the self-study process well. As described in Chapter 1 of this issue, Decoding the Disciplines, pioneered by David Pace and Joan Middendorf, is a process whereby instructors first identify bottlenecks, or "points in a course where the learning of a significant number of students is interrupted" (Anderson 1996 cited by Middendorf and Pace 2004, 4). The next step is for the instructors to engage in a Decoding interview, where two trained interviewers probe to assist the instructor in first clarifying the bottleneck and second, to "reconstruct the steps they themselves do when solving

NEW DIRECTIONS FOR TEACHING AND LEARNING, no. 150, Summer 2017 © 2017 Wiley Periodicals, Inc.
Published online in Wiley Online Library (wileyonlinelibrary.com) • DOI: 10.1002/tl.20240

similar problems" (Middendorf and Pace 2004, 5). AT team members each chose a different bottleneck related to their particular courses and experiences with students. As a group, classroom-based, field-based, and integrative bottlenecks were all represented, but this was not predetermined. Michelle Yeo and Ron MacDonald, two members of the Faculty Learning Community on Decoding the Disciplines at Mount Royal University (see Chapter 1), acted as interviewers for the five members of the AT team, and the interviews were recorded and transcribed. The interviews were conducted as a component of self-study by the AT team, with the interviewees acting as coresearchers, reading and coding the interviews. This process yielded deeper insights than by simply participating in and reflecting on an individual interview. Indeed, the AT team found that the biggest impact came from reading and reflecting upon one another's interviews making this group practice something to consider for the Decoding process more generally.

The transcripts of these interviews reveal thematic support of the framework outlined by Miller-Young and Boman in Chapter 2 of this issue, eliciting similar ways of thinking, ways of practicing, and ways of being. Although the Miller-Young and Boman interviews were conducted across a variety of disciplines, these were concentrated with a group of athletic therapists, and thus the results are compelling to consider in this intradisciplinary context. Although these themes were present within the athletic therapy interviews, additional facets were also evident, which are explored later.

Important insights emerged relating directly to individual classroom practice within the context of the curriculum change in spite of some of the interviewees feeling frustrated at the time of and immediately following the interview. Some overarching insights related to program design, delivery, and structure. Although all of these themes were present to greater or lesser extents across the interviews, each came forward most dramatically in specific cases, and thus within each theme we focus most closely on one or two particular interviews. These themes are described as (1) lifting the veil (or, when the problem is not the problem); (2) the emotional component of learning; (3) unpacking professional intuition in athletic therapy; and finally, (4) disrupting practice in the field. All of these together carry implications for program and curriculum design, and thus, in sum, the chapter offers a practical example of how Decoding work can be used within an academic program to impact program design and delivery.

For the purposes of this chapter, pseudonyms have been given to the interviewees, who were all members of the AT team. All participants are also coresearchers. All are experienced athletic therapists, and they have taught in the athletic therapy program for a range of 6–21 years.

Lifting the Veil (or When the Problem Is Not the Problem)

This theme was particularly prevalent in Julie's interview. Julie chose an apparently straightforward cognitive bottleneck where students had difficulty remembering and being able to identify discs in the spinal column in relation to vertebrae. She initially describes the bottleneck this way:

> There is an anatomical relationship between the nerve roots leaving the back and the disc that would push on it, and students have difficulty in identifying which disc is the one that would actually have the problem. So they can identify what the symptoms are and where it is affected, but they can't identify the cause, the specific location of the cause.

She then goes on to explain the nature of the confusion:

> Throughout the regions of the spine, you have the cervical spine, the thoracic spine and your lumbar spine, and because the size of the vertebra is different in each part of the spine so are the discs and your spinal cord changes ... and so that changes the relationship as well. That is the part that is confusing to people, you can't just say "Oh I have a C5 nerve root symptom, so therefore it is my C5 disc," and in fact it is not that in most cases ... that is where people are having the problem.

> *Interviewer: And what do you do to figure out the next step?*

> Then you go back to your anatomy to understand where does a nerve root exit relative to that disc and vertebra? Like where does it exit the spine? And ... relative to what disc? ... it is more complicated in the lumbar spine because the discs are big and there could be more than one nerve root that is compressed, but it is the weird relationship between where nerve roots exit and disc herniations happen that makes it confusing.

Through the process of the interview, Julie drew the anatomy of the spine and discs on the white board. It was puzzling to the interviewers because the concept itself seemed relatively simple even for disciplinary novices. A key component to understanding the bottleneck emerged as the importance of "drawing it out." Although perhaps tricky to visualize when explained verbally—and certainly Julie uses Powerpoint slides with diagrams as part of her lectures, what came forward was the difference she noted between students who "drew it out" on the margins of their exams when tested on the concept and those who do not:

> I have tried to give them, "Here is how you draw it out for yourself." You can see, and that is interesting to me ... I tend to ask a question or two about it on every exam and the people who generally get it right, many times on the

exam I have seen they have drawn out what I have done or some version of that. Now is it that the people that don't didn't find it helpful? I don't know … or just didn't get it enough to draw it? … but I would say that … not every person who gets it right necessarily drew it, but most do. I don't ask them to draw it, but you see beside the question they have done this little thing for themselves.

The concept of learning through drawing is supported in the learning theory and anatomy teaching literature (Ainsworth, Prain, and Tytler 2011; Balemans et al. 2015; Van Meter and Garner 2005). Despite the fact the concept seems relatively simple to understand, students may be challenged with the material because they were trying to both understand the underlying anatomical theory, while simultaneously trying to integrate this knowledge into the practical application of a clinical presentation such as a "herniated disc," for example. The proverbial juggling of these concepts is often outlined in the cognitive load learning theory literature and drawing the concepts is one of the teaching strategies that has been used successfully to manage the cognitive load on the student (Balemans et al. 2015; McCrudden, McCormick, and McTigue 2011).

Beyond the technical potential discovered of asking her students to "draw-to-learn," through the process of the interview, Julie discovered that the reason for the bottleneck may have less to do with a need to "explain it" better and more to do with a lack of opportunity for the students to apply the information and the assessment processes used to test the learning, whether in the classroom or in a practical setting. Because the events in the clinical or field placements are entirely unpredictable, students are often unlikely to encounter practical learning in a way that neatly synchronizes with their classroom learning. In class, they are often practicing feeling for anatomical structures on one another. However, a common problem in athletic therapy (and indeed in many clinically based programs), is that there is a challenge in providing a practical example at the moment where it would support theoretical learning. Julie explains:

> The problem in class many times is if someone in the class doesn't have something wrong with them we are feeling a whole bunch of normal, and it is not until you feel abnormal that you go, "Ohhh!" like, "I get the difference." We can only hope for people to come in with injuries that we can … people can find that stuff on.

Furthermore, there is a confidence element, which relates as well to the next theme of the emotional component of learning. Julie comments, "I think they do a better job of it than they think that they do, it is having that confidence that I am actually feeling something." A very significant element of the athletic therapy interviews was the kinesthetic, embodied element, of knowing through touch. This relates to Currie's exploration in Chapter 3.

NEW DIRECTIONS FOR TEACHING AND LEARNING • DOI: 10.1002/tl

There was speculation that the technical knowledge itself may not be valued adequately in the field or clinical settings, implying a motivational component. Julie describes how she herself, as a senior student, came to understand the utility of having an in-depth knowledge of anatomy:

> I remember there was an opportunity to take an advanced anatomy class in my last year of school and I ... learned it at a deeper level and I myself had that epiphany of, "Oh my God, how have I been assessing anything thus far?" realizing how poor my anatomy was, or how cobweb covered it was until taking that second course, and having a reason to know it in an applicable way, that, for me, was a very light bulb moment.

Our thinking around teaching underlying theory as knowledge and the separation of this knowledge from the application has evolved considerably over time (Rose and Best 2005). Many professional programs attempt to build clinical competence and in the past, programs separated the theory from the practice in the hope it would transfer naturally. However, as we have come to understand more, the application of theory should be synchronized as part of the overall learning process and when the two are separated or asynchronous, learning may not be optimal (Rose and Best 2005).

What was thought to be a cognitive bottleneck with a simple solution (i.e. "explaining it" better), turned into a different solution whereby students need to focus on the experiences designed to make meaning of the concept, whether theoretically by drawing it out, or experientially, by focusing more on the utility of the concept to practice.

Emotional Component of Learning

As team members engaged in the Decoding process, and drilled down into their own experiences of "a-ha" moments and critical learning, the emotional component to significant learning in the field of athletic therapy became apparent. For several of the team members, significant learning experiences in their own practice were accompanied by powerful emotions such as fear and anxiety. Strong emotions may arise when treating patients and making decisions in front of a stadium of people, or when thinking about the potential harm caused to patients by missing an important step in their evaluation or management process. Events that brought forward these strong emotions often became turning points in their own learning.

In a recent publication, Middendorf et al. (2015) have begun to explore emotional bottlenecks as part of the Decoding process. Although this work is focused upon student learning in the discipline of history, and the role of preexisting ideas and belief systems, their point that "cognitive and affective aspects of learning are intertwined" (169) is relevant to our analysis. All of the chapters of this special issue point toward the important spaces outside of cognitive processes where learning lives, whether that is Miller-Young and Boman's ways of practicing and ways of being, Currie's notions of embodiment, or Yeo's hermeneutic dialogic relationship between the discipline and the world (Chapters 2, 3, and 4).

In the case of the athletic therapy students, the emotional aspects of their learning come less from epistemological assumptions or preconceptions and more to do with the immediate emotions raised by situations creating enormous pressure and anxiety, interpersonal challenges such as telling a coach a valued player cannot return to the game or fear in a clinical setting of harming a patient. These sorts of bottlenecks to learning surfaced in all of the interviews, but most strikingly in Jason's. He explains how this learning process was for him as a developing professional, as he begins to consider how to embed this learning for his students:

> That is not something that we teach—something blatant that we teach... people are going to be yelling at you and you have to gather as much information as you can so you can explain it to the person... but then how do you manage a situation where all that stuff is going on and you have to focus on one person? Someone is yelling in your ear... It really clicked home the first time I had to go on court and it was like, "I am actually focusing!"... I can feel my heart racing, I am a little nervous, but I am actually talking to the patient, which is good. And in that same example, we took the patient over to the bench and having to explain to the coach why they weren't able to go back in... So I bumbled around my words and I kind of gave too much irrelevant information when all I had to say was, "He can't play..." That was one of the experiences that kind of helped me learn to... just stick with the relevant stuff.

The role of experience for the novice in moving through difficult emotional bottlenecks in professional education cannot be overemphasized. The question for the instructional team became then how to intentionally support such learning experiences. Part of the answer seems to be becoming much more explicit in the classroom in terms of an instructor's own experiences as an athletic therapist: how they themselves encountered and navigated such powerful emotional bottlenecks (also see MacDonald, Chapter 5).

Unpacking "Professional Intuition" in Athletic Therapy

All of the interviews raised the concept of tacit knowledge in athletic therapy, in the intuition or gut-level expertise. Different team members expressed this in different ways. All of the interviews discussed the observational skills, the "ways of seeing" that athletic therapists develop, along with interview skills, manual skills, and the ability to follow a decision tree or other mental structures in order to arrive at the correct diagnosis and

New Directions for Teaching and Learning • DOI: 10.1002/tl

treatment. A common theme was the role of extensive experience and re-flection in the practice of the AT instructors. The interviews delved into how complex this is for students, the need to break things down for them, and the struggle and strategies the instructors pursue in order to make the im-plicit explicit. This theme came forward most strongly in Erica's and Kelly's interviews.

Erica explains the bottleneck this way:

> They get so burnt out and they are just like, "Just tell me the list. What is the list that I have to do in order to get through this?" And rehab doesn't have a list; it has a bubble that you try and put together... I think at the end of the day it is so hard for them to have to integrate everything in a high volume program.

Similarly, Kelly explains, "So it is putting it all together and I find... that they have each of the pieces of the puzzle and it is putting it together that is the biggest bottleneck." In their own practice, all of the instructors describe an incredibly complex process of analysis and decision making. When probed, they describe how they begin their assessment the moment they have visual contact with a patient in the clinic, as Kelly describes, "So we are looking for any signs and symptoms like swelling, bruising, deformi-ties, and you are also observing when they came in, are they limping? Are they kind of favoring and babying an area?" In a field context Jason is incor-porating his knowledge of the sport, the field conditions, and an intensive observation of the play such that he will usually actually see the injury oc-cur. Each instructor describes the importance of gathering a proper history, but this process is highly flexible and requires judgment throughout. Erica points out, "If you take a good history you have 80 percent of your answer about the person from the history alone... then as you go through all the physical testing you are basically testing your theory." Kelly explains,

> They are set questions but they are always geared and pinpointed toward my conversation with you right? So I am going to start a conversation and I know I have all these questions I am supposed to ask in a basket and I don't ask them if I know that I don't need to ask them, and I am not always doing it in a rote manner, right? Because... I am at the point now where I can have a conversation and lead it.

In analyzing the transcripts, instructors began to wonder about a kind of mythology that may develop of "magical" experts, a perception that ath-letic therapists "just know." Students perceiving this myth may become in-timidated or overwhelmed by experts' tacit processes that appear impossible to decode for themselves. Students watch experienced therapists apparently skip over steps in practice, yet the consensus is for the expert that one must do each step in sequence for many, many repetitions before the process becomes internalized. When asked what they do when they encounter something they haven't seen before, each instructor describes a process whereby they go back to basics and slow down the steps, and they are quick to consult with other experts as part of their process. In making these processes explicit for themselves, an opportunity is created to make this more explicit for students.

Disrupting Practice in the Field

An interesting tension appearing in the interviews was the relationship between the field of practice and the academic program. This tension is very common across many professional programs, where students experience theoretical learning on campus integrated with clinical experiences (Rose and Best 2005). Although instructors in the athletic therapy program engage in professional practice themselves, there is still often a tension between the field and its perception of the university and the "ivory tower" as contrasted with "practical knowledge." Students will naturally default to the way things are taught in the "real world" of the field. From the program perspective, instructors can also become frustrated by the gap between contemporary literature and research and current practice in the field. In working with students, for example, in Paul's interview on identifying the correct level for ultrasound, there is a, sometimes unspoken, hope that the students might become positive disruptive influences in the field. He comments,

> I have seen probably three generations of students who have gone through under a mentor and they all use a cookbook approach, "We will use it at 1.0 watts per square centimeter for 5 minutes." For what? For everything! And that is totally wrong to use a preset, and yet everyone does it in the industry.

Paul identifies the complexity of determining the correct level for ultrasound as a complex bottleneck for students, but further, this is compounded in the field where students do not see it done correctly by practitioners. Paul explains, "I think they just don't value it because they hear people in the industry say, 'Who cares, it doesn't really matter.... Ultrasound is useless,' and yeah, the truth of it is the way you are doing it is useless, but if you do it properly it is actually quite useful." The hope for disruptive influence occurs when "what you are trying to teach them that is more sophisticated than what you see in the field." Through the process of the Decoding interview, Paul began to expand on this notion:

> We don't want to create... we are not trying to educate technicians, we are trying to educate critical thinkers... that is why we are in this problem with ultrasound, why so many people do it wrong because we have educated technicians in the past and they just followed a recipe.... I know I want to make a change in the way people practice... I want them to make decisions.

NEW DIRECTIONS FOR TEACHING AND LEARNING • DOI: 10.1002/tl

This idea came forward in several of the interviews in different ways. Professional programs rely on the practical knowledge of clinical or practicum placements in order for students to have the opportunity for critical experiential learning. Yet, a tension is created when the practice modeled in the field is not always "best practice" as conceptualized by the program. At the same time, practitioners can become frustrated if they feel university instructors are out of touch with the real world of practice. This tension lives itself out in the learning of the students, who do not always know how to understand or work within this tension productively. Students are seeking clear guidance and guidelines in what for them are potentially intimidating contexts, where they are asked to perform skills they are only just beginning to develop, and integrate theory and practice in a complex decision-making processes.

Program and Curriculum Design, Curriculum, Delivery, and Structure

All of these insights fed directly into decision making within the program and fueled further discussion and inquiry. At the time of this writing, a second phase of the study is underway about the impact of the new curricular approach on student learning. The AT team will be collecting longitudinal data from students as they progress through the program.

There are a number of curricular delivery outcomes that have resulted from the Decoding experience. The course sequencing and laddering of the curriculum was evident before the experience but has been significantly reinforced by the experience. For example, it was critical to design the program in such a manner that practical experiences (formal tutorial and practicum courses) are scheduled simultaneously in the same semester so students could see the theory and practice links. Furthermore, it helped to design individual lessons whereby the theory was complemented and reinforced by practical learning activities in either the lecture or the accompanying tutorial. Again, bottlenecks in student learning are often thought of as merely cognitive in nature, but they may also be motivational whereby students see connections and relevance of theory only when there is a very specific practical outcome associated with them. The team began to think about the notion of experience versus education, for example, the difference between depending upon chance exposures in the field, versus thoughtful, simulated, or intentional real-life exposure with application and debriefing, based on specific learning objectives. The former is wishful thinking, the latter is mindful. Finally, it became clear that there is a need for careful professional development for clinical instructors to increase awareness of their own tacit knowledge, helping them to articulate the implicit as they work with students.

New Directions for Teaching and Learning • DOI: 10.1002/tl

References

Ainsworth, Shaaron, Vaughan Prain, and Russell Tytler. 2011. "Science Education. Drawing to Learn in Science." *Science* 333 (6046): 1096–1097. https://doi.org/10.1126/science.1204153.

Balemans, Monique C. M., Jan G. M. Kooloos, A. Rogier T. Donders, and Catharina E. E. M. Van der Zee. 2015. "Actual Drawing of Histological Images Improves Knowledge Retention." *Anatomical Sciences Education* 9 (1): 60–70. https://doi.org/10.1002/ase.1545.

Lafave, Mark, Michelle Yeo, Khatija Westbrook, Dennis Valdez, Breda Eubank, and Jenelle McAllister,. 2016. "Content Validation of Athletic Therapy Clinical Presentations in Canada." *Athletic Training Education Journal* 11 (2): 82-87.

McCrudden, Matthew T., Montana K. McCormick, and Erin M. McTigue. 2011. "Do the Spatial Features of an Adjunct Display That Readers Complete While Reading Affect Their Understanding of a Complex System?" *International Journal of Science and Mathematics Education* 9: 163–185. 10.1007/s10763-010-9236-1.

Middendorf, Joan, Jolants Mickute, Tara Saunders, José Najar, Andrew E. Clark-Huckstep, David Pace, with Keith Eberly and Nicole McGrath. 2015. "What's Feeling Got to Do with It? Decoding Emotional Bottlenecks in the History Classroom." *Arts and Humanities in Higher Education* 14 (2): 166–180.

Middendorf, Joan, and David Pace. 2004. "Decoding the Disciplines: A Model for Helping Students Learn Disciplinary Ways of Thinking." In *New Directions in Teaching and Learning: No. 98. Decoding the Disciplines: Helping Students Learn Disciplinary Ways of Thinking*, edited by David Pace and Joan Middendorf, 1–11. San Francisco: Jossey-Bass.

Rose, Miranda, and Dawn Best. 2005. *Transforming Practice Through Clinical Education, Professional Supervision, and Mentoring*. Amsterdam: Elsevier Health Sciences.

Van Meter, Peggy, and Joanna Garner. 2005. "The Promise and Practice of Learner-Generated Drawing: Literature Review and Synthesis." *Educational Psychology Review* 17 (4): 285–325. 10.1007/s10648-005-8136-3.

Yeo, Michelle, Mark Lafave, Khatija Westbrook, Dennis Valdez, Breda Eubank, and Jenelle McAllister. 2016. Curricular change: Deepening professional community. *Transformative Dialogues* 9 (1): 1-12.

MICHELLE YEO *has been a faculty developer and faculty member in Mount Royal University's Academic Development Centre since 2007.*

MARK R LAFAVE *is a professor and certified athletic therapist. He has been at Mount Royal University since 1994.*

KHATIJA WESTBROOK *has been a faculty member in the Department of Health and Physical Education at Mount Royal University since 2005.*

JENELLE MCALLISTER *has been a faculty member in the Mount Royal University Health and Physical Education Department since 2006.*

DENNIS VALDEZ *is an assistant professor in the Department of Health and Physical Education at Mount Royal University. As a certified athletic therapist he serves as a field practicum supervisor and practitioner.*

BREDA EUBANK *has been a faculty member at Mount Royal University's Health and Physical Education Department since 2009.*

NEW DIRECTIONS FOR TEACHING AND LEARNING • DOI: 10.1002/tl

8

This final chapter synthesizes the findings and implications derived from applying the Decoding the Disciplines model across disciplines and within communities of practice. We make practical suggestions for teachers and researchers who wish to apply and extend this work.

Learning from Decoding across Disciplines and within Communities of Practice

Janice Miller-Young, Jennifer Boman

We suggested at the beginning of this issue that the Decoding the Disciplines model not only provides a framework for inquiry into teaching and learning disciplinary concepts but also holds much potential for bridging thinking and teaching practice *across* disciplines. The chapters subsequently presented have extended the Decoding model in several ways, using it for epistemological and ontological bottlenecks. By analyzing interviews about seven bottlenecks from diverse disciplines, we uncovered common themes that illustrate experts' ways of thinking, practicing, and being (Chapter 2, this issue). For example, these expert approaches required not only the ability to perform tasks such as deconstructing problems and recognizing patterns but also the confidence to take agency in pursuing knowledge and to take time to explore different perspectives before coming to a decision. These ways of thinking, being, and practicing were employed even when thinking through concepts that our interviewees initially thought were relatively "simple" cognitive bottlenecks. Also, by analyzing these interviews through different theoretical lenses, we have proposed in this chapter several new lines of questioning for use in Decoding interviews. Finally, by applying the Decoding interview within two different communities of practice we have shown how it can influence both teaching and curriculum. In all cases, we have been struck by the power of the Decoding interview in revealing basic assumptions about disciplinary thinking as well as the role it can play in developing the community and trust necessary for collaborative teaching and/or research projects.

Implications for Teaching and Curriculum

Use of the Decoding framework has much potential as a tool to help close the gap between expert and novice thinking. As Middendorf and Pace

NEW DIRECTIONS FOR TEACHING AND LEARNING, no. 150, Summer 2017 © 2017 Wiley Periodicals, Inc.
Published online in Wiley Online Library (wileyonlinelibrary.com) • DOI: 10.1002/tl.20241

(2004) indicate, making disciplinary operations explicit and finding ways to model these can help move students toward mastery and success. We have suggested in this special issue that the benefits of Decoding can be realized both at an individual teacher level as well as across programs and curricula. We raise the following three implications for teaching and curriculum based on this work.

Teacher Reflection.   Looking at patterns in teachers' tacit thinking within and across disciplines can help provide a starting point for understanding one's own hidden assumptions and beliefs. The themes illustrated across this issue provide a number of specific ideas for teachers to reflect on—from common themes related to expert ways of thinking, practicing, and being (Miller-Young and Boman, Chapter 2), or the role of lived experience and embodiment in one's practice (Currie, Chapter 3), to deepening our understanding of how students experience our disciplines (Yeo, Chapter 4).

In particular, the role of experience, which ultimately led to experts' confidence and seemingly intuitive ways of thinking, emerged as a strong theme across all chapters. Our findings highlighted the importance of instructors becoming more conscious of how their experience helped to develop their expertise and thinking more purposefully about how to support such learning experiences for our students. Articulating these reflections could help us to be more explicit about our own experiences with our students. As MacDonald (Chapter 5) suggests, telling our own *stories* of learning and identity development may be another strategy to improve students' experience by reducing affective bottlenecks such as those that were strongly evident in the interviews with athletic therapy instructors (Yeo et al., Chapter 7).

The literature suggests that keeping journals, thinking deeply about our teaching, and considering feedback from students and colleagues are important ways for faculty to critically reflect on our ways of practicing and further, that reflecting on and sharing our own educational *stories* can help us understand what we bring to our work (Shadiow 2013). We suggest the Decoding interview could be added to this list of strategies. We found the Decoding interview, even when the interviewee is not involved in the research project, to be a powerful tool to help faculty become more conscious or, and thus able to critically reflect on, an aspect of their practice (Currie, Chapter 3, this issue; Haney 2015). In the words of Yeo (Chapter 4), this kind of inquiry could open us up to being more generous with our students; to not only being focused on explaining concepts better, but being "focused on understanding the students better and how they are experiencing the discipline."

Supportive Communities.   Whereas others have emphasized the importance of reflecting on one's own Decoding efforts within a supportive community (Middendorf and Shopkow 2017), we have also shown how reflecting on *others'* interviews within a community of practice can challenge our assumptions and generate new insights. The service-learning (Chapter 6) and athletic therapy (Chapter 7) communities of practice both conducted collaborative self-studies in connection with Decoding, which seems to have played a powerful role in the impact of the interviews. As the service-learning group reported elsewhere, the Decoding interview itself can be important to the functioning of a collaborative learning community because it can help generate a climate of trust (Miller-Young et al. 2015), which is important when we are confronting the risks of learning and changing. Together, these findings suggest that Decoding has much potential for further use in professional development as well as research initiatives.

Curriculum Development.   Students need time to integrate the disciplinary knowledge they are learning with disciplinary ways of practicing and being. However, ways of thinking, practicing, and being are not often considered in curriculum planning. As we write in Chapter 2, "we might consider whether our teaching decontextualizes knowledge from the practices to which it relates, whether we prioritize content and 'efficiency of transmission' over deep understanding, and whether we focus on epistemology and narrow conceptions of knowledge at the expense of ontology . . . these themes could inform curriculum planning and related teaching and learning research in one's course, program, or discipline." As one example, the athletic therapy program has become more intentional about designing practical learning activities in lectures and tutorials rather than leaving students' experiential learning to chance exposures in clinical or practicum placements (Yeo et al., Chapter 7).

Implications for Decoding

Although the scholarship of teaching and learning started with a focus on students' learning and learning processes (Kreber and Cranton 2000), the field has evolved to include a range of methodologies and epistemologies (Miller-Young and Yeo 2015; Poole 2013) and recognizes the need to address discipline-centered "ways of thinking, feeling, and behaving" (Coppola and Krajcik 2013, 628) as well as common goals such as critical thinking (Middendorf and Shopkow 2017). There are several new ways Decoding could be used to address these topics.

Extending the Model.   Although traditionally the focus of the Decoding interview has been on cognitive or procedural bottlenecks, our interviews with disciplinary experts also explored what could be considered epistemological and ontological bottlenecks (Miller-Young and Boman, Chapter 2). In doing so, we also suggested new lines of questioning for Decoding interviews based on both our intuitive exploration and the use of different theoretical lenses. For example, Currie (Chapter 3) proposed the addition of sensory and experiential questions, Yeo (Chapter 4) put forward questions about how experts interpret texts, their orientation to questions, and sense of play, whereas MacDonald (Chapter 5) indicated how narrative identity theories might be used to help interviewers focus on uncovering and translating our disciplinary identities. It will be useful to further explore the utility of these lenses and questions in Decoding interviews, particularly for such noncognitive bottlenecks, and to examine the impact of extending the interview in this manner for both the instructor and, ultimately, his or her students.

Decoding Nonexperts.   Although the premise behind the Decoding framework is to help make expert thinking visible, we have also explored Decoding of faculty members who were *not* experts on the bottleneck (i.e., reciprocity in service-learning) and discovered the utility of the Decoding interview, followed by critical reflection, to generate new learning and influence their teaching practice. This potential should be further explored for other contexts and participants. As one example, these findings suggest that conducting Decoding interviews with novices such as students throughout their development as learners in a discipline or program would also be a productive avenue to explore.

Future Work

In this special issue, we have shown how Decoding is one tool to help us uncover and translate our disciplines, our experiences, and our ways of thinking, being, and practicing for our students. We have also suggested ways to extend this tool through theoretical lenses, new lines of questioning, and communities of practice. As such, it will be important to intentionally inquire into the effectiveness of these suggested strategies in helping to uncover our disciplines for our students.

Although this issue has largely focused on the role of the Decoding interview, it is also valuable to consider the subsequent steps in the Decoding model, particularly how to use our learning from Decoding to improve how we give feedback to students and assess their learning. For example, the athletic therapy team is continuing their study by collecting longitudinal data from students as they progress through the revised program, and Rathburn and Lexier from the service-learning group are collecting data about students' understanding of service-learning and will be able to compare similar data sets from before and after their Decoding self-study.

Teaching and learning are multifaceted phenomena, and knowledge is "in part a product of the activity, context, and culture in which it is developed and used" (Brown, Collins, and Duguid 1989, 32). With this in mind, we have identified several possibilities to further the use of Decoding in innovative and influential ways. We hope this issue, together with several other Decoding resources recently available (Middendorf and Shopkow, 2017; Pace 2017), provides the resources and inspiration for others from diverse backgrounds to experiment with the framework in their own contexts in order to improve teaching and learning, build communities of practice, and contribute valuable scholarship that informs and transforms higher education.

References

Brown, John Seely, Allan Collins, and Paul Duguid. 1989. "Situated Cognition and the Culture of Learning." *Educational Researcher* 18 (1): 32–42.

Coppola, Brian P., and Joseph S. Krajcik. 2013. "Discipline-Centered Post-Secondary Science Education Research: Understanding University Level Science Learning." *Journal of Research in Science Teaching* 50 (6): 627–638.

Haney, Sally. 2015. "Interrogating Our Past Practice as We Scale the Walls of the Box We Call Journalism Education." In *Toward 2020: New Directions in Journalism Education*, edited by Gene Allen, Stephanie Craft, Christopher Waddell, and Mary Lynn Young, 64–81. Toronto: Ryerson Journalism Research Centre.

Kreber, Carolin, and Patricia A. Cranton. 2000. "Exploring the Scholarship of Teaching." *Journal of Higher Education* 71 (4): 476–495.

Middendorf, Joan, and David Pace. 2004. "Decoding the Disciplines: A Model for Helping Students Learn Disciplinary Ways of Thinking." In *New Directions in Teaching and Learning: No. 98. Decoding the Disciplines: Helping Students Learn Disciplinary Ways of Thinking*, edited by David Pace and Joan Middendorf, 1–11. San Francisco: Jossey-Bass.

Middendorf, Joan, and Leah Shopkow, eds. 2017. *Decoding the Disciplines: How to Help Students Learn Critical Thinking*. Bloomington, IN: Indiana University Press.

Miller-Young, Janice, and Michelle Yeo. 2015. "Conceptualizing and Communicating SoTL: A Framework for the Field." *Teaching and Learning Inquiry* 3 (2): 37–53.

Miller-Young, Janice, Yasmin Dean, Melanie Rathburn, Jennifer Pettit, Margot Underwood, Judy Gleeson, Roberta Lexier, Victoria Calvert, and Patti Clayton. 2015. "Decoding Ourselves: An Inquiry into Faculty Learning About Reciprocity in Service-Learning." *Michigan Journal of Community Service Learning* 22 (1): 32–47.

Pace, David. 2017. *The Decoding the Disciplines Paradigm: Seven Steps to Increased Student Learning*. Bloomington, IN: Indiana University Press.

Poole, Gary. 2013. "Square One: What Is Research." In *The Scholarship of Teaching and Learning in and across the Disciplines*, edited by Kathleen McKinney, 135–151. Bloomington, IN: Indiana University Press.

Shadiow, Linda K. 2013. *What Our Stories Teach Us: A Guide to Critical Reflection for College Faculty*. San Francisco: Jossey-Bass.

JANICE MILLER-YOUNG *is a professor and the academic chair of the Centre for Teaching and Learning at the University of Alberta.*

JENNIFER BOMAN *has been a faculty developer and faculty member in Mount Royal University's Academic Development Centre since 2010.*

NEW DIRECTIONS FOR TEACHING AND LEARNING • DOI: 10.1002/tl

INDEX

Affective Learning Project (ALP), 65
Ainsworth, S., 90
Annells, M., 41, 43
Ardizzone, T., 19
Athletic therapy (AT), 87, 92–94

Baillie, C., 20
Balemans, M. C. M., 90
Bergum, V., 38
Bernstein, J., 77
Best, D., 91, 94
Boman, J., 7, 13, 15, 16, 18, 19, 35, 37, 39, 57, 63, 88, 97, 98, 99, 101
Bourdieu, P., 46
Bozalek, V., 78
Bransford, J. D., 31, 32
Breithaupt, F., 19
Bringle, R. G., 76, 78, 80
Brockmeier, J., 69
Brown, A. L., 31, 32
Brown, J. S., 100
Brown, P. C., 32
Burbules, N. C., 64
Burke, P. J., 70
Burke-Stets system, 70
Burkholder, J. P., 77
Burn, K., 33

Calvert, V., 17, 20, 75–81, 83, 85, 99
Carbaugh, D., 69
Chung, T.-T., 77
Church, M., 14
Clark-Huckstep, A. E., 20, 65, 91
Clayton, P., 17, 20, 76, 77, 79, 99
Clayton, P. H., 76, 78, 80
Cocking, R. R., 31, 32
Cole, R., 83
Collins, A., 100
Coppola, B. P., 99
Cousin, G., 20
Cranton, P. A., 99
Cross, N., 32
Curriculum development, 99. *See also* Decoding across disciplines, learning from
Currie, G., 13, 18, 33, 37, 48, 98, 99

Dall'Alba, G., 32, 64
Dean, Y., 17, 20, 75, 76, 77, 79, 80, 83, 85, 99
Dear, S., 77
Decoding across disciplines, learning from, 97; future prospects, 100–101; implications for decoding, 99–100; teaching and curriculum, 97–99
Decoding disciplinary identities, 63–64; decoding identity, 71–72; identity and learning, 64–65; identity theory, 68–71; professional identities, 65–68; sociological components, 70
Decoding interview, 63
Decoding interview to teaching practice, building bridges from, 75–76; background and methods, 76–78; impact of decoding self-study, 78–83
Decoding learning community, 16
Decoding model, applications of, 16–17
Decoding nonexperts, 100
Decoding the disciplines, 19–21; background and purpose of study, 21; findings, 23–31; implications, 31–33; methods, 21–23
Decoding work, impact of, 87–91; athletic therapy, 92–94; disrupting practice, 94–95; emotional component of learning, 91–92; program and curriculum design, 95
Dialogical self theory, 70–71
Díaz, A., 14, 19, 63, 77
Disciplines, phenomenology and decoding the, 37–38; decoding interviews, 38–40; embodied knowing, 43–45; implications for educators, 45–47; inquiry, 38; practicing and disciplinary knowledge, 40–41; prereflective practice, 41–42
Donders, A. R. T., 90
Dorrestijn, M., 83
Drevdahl, D. J., 77
Driscoll, A., 14
Duguid, P., 100

50 Techniques for Engaging Students and Assessing Learning in College Courses

ELIZABETH F. BARKLEY
CLAIRE HOWELL MAJOR

LEARNING ASSESSMENT TECHNIQUES

A HANDBOOK FOR COLLEGE FACULTY

JOSSEY-BASS
A Wiley Brand

Do you want to:

- Know what and how well your students are learning?

- Promote active learning in ways that readily integrate assessment?

- Gather information that can help make grading more systematic and streamlined?

- Efficiently collect solid learning outcomes data for institutional assessment?

- Provide evidence of your teaching effectiveness for promotion and tenure review?

"An expertly documented, superbly organized, and convincingly written book centered around 50 techniques that showcase the power of course-based, teacher-driven, integrated assessment. It's the sequel to *Classroom Assessment Techniques* we've all been waiting for and it doesn't disappoint."

Maryellen Weimer, professor emerita, Penn State, and editor, *The Teaching Professor* newsletter and blog

Also available as an e-book.

JOSSEY-BASS™
A Wiley Brand

Jossey-Bass is a registered trademark of John Wiley & Sons. Inc.

Small changes that make a big difference

"*Small Teaching* offers what so many faculty members want and need: small-scale changes that can enhance their teaching and their students' learning— not just 'someday' but Monday."

Marsha C. Lovett, director, Eberly Center for Teaching Excellence & Educational Innovation, Carnegie Mellon University, and coauthor, *How Learning Works*

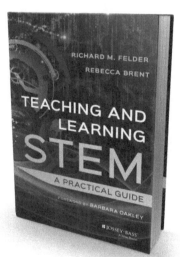

"Felder and Brent, longtime leaders in STEM education research, fill an important gap by providing both insightful and very practical guidance for the college instructor trying to translate the findings of STEM research into effective classroom practice."

Carl Wieman, Nobel Laureate in Physics, Department of a Physics and Graduate School of Education, Stanford University

e Also available as e-books.

Jossey-Bass is a registered trademark of John Wiley & Sons, Inc.

JB JOSSEY-BASS™
A Wiley Brand

NEW DIRECTIONS FOR TEACHING AND LEARNING
ORDER FORM SUBSCRIPTION AND SINGLE ISSUES

DISCOUNTED BACK ISSUES:

Use this form to receive 20% off all back issues of *New Directions for Teaching and Learning*.
All single issues priced at **$23.20** (normally $29.00)

TITLE	ISSUE NO.	ISBN

Call 1-800-835-6770 or see mailing instructions below. When calling, mention the promotional code JBNND to receive your discount. For a complete list of issues, please visit www.wiley.com/WileyCDA/WileyTitle/productCd-TL.html

SUBSCRIPTIONS: (1 YEAR, 4 ISSUES)

☐ New Order   ☐ Renewal

U.S.	☐ Individual: $89	☐ Institutional: $356
CANADA/MEXICO	☐ Individual: $89	☐ Institutional: $398
ALL OTHERS	☐ Individual: $113	☐ Institutional: $434

Call 1-800-835-6770 or see mailing and pricing instructions below.
Online subscriptions are available at www.onlinelibrary.wiley.com

ORDER TOTALS:

Issue / Subscription Amount: $ _____

Shipping Amount: $ _____
(for single issues only – subscription prices include shipping)

Total Amount: $ _____

SHIPPING CHARGES:

First Item $6.00
Each Add'l Item $2.00

(No sales tax for U.S. subscriptions. Canadian residents, add GST for subscription orders. Individual rate subscriptions must be paid by personal check or credit card. Individual rate subscriptions may not be resold as library copies.)

BILLING & SHIPPING INFORMATION:

☐ **PAYMENT ENCLOSED:** *(U.S. check or money order only. All payments must be in U.S. dollars.)*

☐ **CREDIT CARD:** ☐ VISA ☐ MC ☐ AMEX

Card number _____Exp. Date_____

Card Holder Name_____Card Issue #_____

Signature _____Day Phone_____

☐ **BILL ME:** *(U.S. institutional orders only. Purchase order required.)*

Purchase order # _____
Federal Tax ID 13559302 • GST 89102-8052

Name_____

Address_____

Phone_____ E-mail_____

Copy or detach page and send to: **John Wiley & Sons, Inc. / Jossey Bass**
PO Box 55381
Boston, MA 02205-9850

PROMO JBNND